The View from Foley Mountain

Here is a celebration of the joy of living in harmony with the natural world ... of pleasures once taken for granted, now becoming less familiar. The seasonal selections lead you through the fields, woods, rock outcroppings and shores of the conservation area which are the author's home.

You will savour the fragrance of maple syrup boiling, share in a summer heron census, snow shoe to a beaver lodge, watch a snapping turtle laying eggs, witness the death of a starving deer, and see turkey vultures soar.

Whether she is rejoicing in old barns, canoeing the Snake River, harvesting dye plants or stalking moths at night, Peri McQuay's deep love and lyrical vision stimulates you to share her sense of wonder in her surroundings.

You will want to keep a copy of *The View from Foley Mountain* on your bedside table, at the cottage, or in your packsack, to be dipped into at your leisure.

Writer and countrywoman, Peri McQuay, grew up in the woods in Mississauga with a deep love of nature and literature. She lives with her teacher/conservationist husband and their two sons in Foley Mountain Conservation Area, north of Kingston.

The View from Foley Mountain

PERI PHILLIPS McQUAY

with line drawings by Jillian Gilliland

NATURAL HERITAGE / NATURAL HISTORY INC.

The author gratefully acknowledges permission to quote from
Dylan Thomas, *The Poems,* published by J.M. Dent, London,
England. Permission granted by David Higham Associates
Limited. Much of the contents of this book has appeared
previously in the *Whig-Standard, Bird Watcher's Digest* and
The Snowy Egret.

The View from Foley Mountain by Peri Phillips McQuay

First published by Butternut Press, Westport, Ont. 1987.
Published 1995 by Natural Heritage / Natural History Inc.
P.O. Box 95, Station "O", Toronto, Ontario M4A 2M8

Design and typsetting: Robin Brass Studio
Printed and bound in Canada by Hignell Printing Limited,
Winnipeg, Manitoba

The cover painting is by Marie Cecilia Guard, and permission
to reproduce it is granted by Lisa Moses.

Canadian Cataloguing in Publication Data

McQuay, Peri Phillips, 1945–
     The view from Foley Mountain

ISBN 0-920474-99-3

1. Foley Mountain Conservation Area (Ont.).
2. McQuay, Peri Phillips, 1945–   . 3. Nature.
I. Title

QH77.C3M37 1995   508.71373   C95-930743-5

Natural Heritage / Natural History Inc. gratefully
acknowledges the assistance of the Canada Council, the
Ontario Arts Council, and the Government of Ontario
through the Ministry of Culture, Tourism and Recreation.

For my parents, Marie and Ken Phillips,
and my husband, Barry McQuay,
who have enriched my view immeasurably

Acknowledgements

In this new edition, I would particularly like to offer my warmest thanks to all my readers who help me stay connected with the heart of life.

I also would like to thank those at the Rideau Valley Conservation Authority who have ensured the preservation of what is special at Foley Mountain.

My gratitude goes out to those who helped my early writing into print, the people at the *Whig-Standard* who made the column and essays of *The View from Foley Mountain* possible, particularly Roger Bainbridge and Sheldon MacNeil, who gave me my first encouragement, and Dave McGill of Butternut Press and editor Betty Jane Corson, along with illustrator-friend Jillian Gilliland.

Finally, my sincere appreciation to Barry Penhale of Natural Heritage / Natural History Inc. for making this new edition of *The View from Foley Mountain* available.

Contents

At home today

Welcome. Someday, after you've climbed the big hill on the highway going north towards Perth, you may notice stone gates and a rustic sign announcing the Foley Mountain Conservation Area. The cloud of pines and a winding lane invite and you may turn off the highway, curious to see what happens after the early bend in the road.

If you walk on down the light-dappled road you may be tempted to stop when you reach the sign for Spy Rock. You may even follow the short, rocky path to this landmark through dark trees and out onto the scraped granite bones of "the Mountain". Here you can see a world within itself: lake, fields, the sugar bush over on the hill, the village, and, if you know how to look, the life within it all.

The light on Spy Rock is bright, though, and you may remember that the lane goes on through the shady woods. Will you see my favourite yellow birch, I wonder, with its shaggy bark glistening in the sun? Listen, deeper in the woods the pileated woodpecker is drilling. If you came with me I could show you his tree. There are footprints on the road if you look down, telling shadowy stories of the passers by – here the heelmarks of an early morning raccoon, there the heart-shaped prints of a fawn. There are tire tracks, too, in the dust of the lane, and yet, only twenty minutes away from there I could take you to places where no one has walked for years, perhaps forever.

If you continue following the curves and rises, the little road leaves the woods and cuts through the fields of the old farm. Here again you have a choice. Ahead, the road continues across the park's eight hundred wild acres, past beaver ponds, trails and winter deer yards until it turns steeply downhill, past the sometime waterfall and ends at the lake.

If you've the time, though, turn aside for a few minutes and follow the short road to the left that leads to my home. Will you see only rough, overgrown fields in a lonely landscape, or will you be able to see the view as it seems to me when I swing into the lane returning home from an extended ramble?

You really should stop when you come to Morgan's willow-circled pond. As my elder son has known since he was very little, there's more going on in and around ponds than anywhere else in the park. In spring, at least, there's just enough water in this one to catch sky and wind-ripples. You're almost certain to glimpse the resident pair of blue-winged teals before they slip in amongst the willows, and there, flashing among the pollen-heavy catkins is the yellow warbler, almost too canary-coloured for a northern scene. As you pass the floating log, scan the sunning turtles closely. Amongst the reptilian ecstasy may well be one of our rare, dome-shelled Blandings turtles.

If you haven't been mesmerized by the swirl of the whirligig beetles, move on slowly up the rise towards the house. Pause to admire the bees' dance in the "beeloud glade" I made for them, then look up into the sky where the turkey vultures drift. There's so much to see. It's a good thing you've come.

At the end of the road the door to my farmhouse home is open. Look in for a moment. Depending on the day, I'm afraid, the fragrance may be baking bread or my husband Barry's pet skunk Fanny. I often wish I could know what a visitor sees through the open door. What will you make of the wasp nest swinging from the ceiling over Barry's big banker's desk or the African mud paintings on the wall? The music room, just off to the side barely holds a couch and a rocking chair, yet somehow we've made room for a large old long-stringed piano and a parlour organ. It gets better, or worse, depending on your point of view, if you round the corner. Here I have my floor loom set up, and possibly a spinning wheel or two in evidence. They compliment the rustic skunk cage. What else? Well, this is a house where books ebb and flow like Dickensian dust heaps. There is a continual war for wall space between the book shelves and the paintings and drawings my artist parents have given me. It now appears that my only future recourse will be to build bookshelves on the ceiling.

If you've been standing here long enough to take in all of this, you've almost certainly been greeted by at least some of the four members of the cat tribe we support. One member of the tribe tends to sit on visitors'shoulders, giving precedence to those who dislike cats, so we'll hope that she, at least, is out walking.

You may have noticed that this is a house where inside and out are unusually loosely defined. The inside windowsills are filled with a jungle of plants and outside a lilac scrapes the screen and hummingbirds beckon.

Although I had very little previous experience with boys before my two sons, Morgan and Jeremy, I've resigned myself wholeheartedly to the species as is also evident. I decided a long time ago, that if we were all going to survive, my standards would have to be lowered (not altogether a loss, I've found). Hence, the lopsided couchcover and hallway litter of fishing rods, boots for all seasons, baseball gloves, snakeskins, hawk feathers and hammers left over from the long defunct McQuay Brothers' summer woodworking shop.

A long time ago, exasperated friends looked around the loosely organized chaos resulting from our many interests. Genuinely worried that we might be frittering our lives away, they suggested we "get our priorities straight". We disagreed then, and still do. Visits to more orderly, simpler homes leave us feeling homesick. How does someone manage without ladybugs and spiders to observe on the darkest winter days? How could one settle to read one book when five are so much more rewarding? How could we abandon the scraggy scented geraniums that have travelled all over Ontario with us? Each of the several cats compliments the others. Always, as we survey piles of tools or surplus books, we are mindful that nearly anything might come in handy sometime.

Well, let's leave the house. I hope you'll want to come back later. There's so much to talk about. Meanwhile, I want you to see our gardens. I could apologize endlessly for their shortcomings: the droughts, the soil ... I always intended to have drifts of flowers, and rows of vegetables. Instead, I've settled for evocation. Seasoned with imagination, I can get as much pleasure from my few antique roses as a professional does from a bank of them. Even one flower has many stories, and if the combinations sometimes are felicitous as well, so much the better.

Our old friend Stan Crawford gave us the vegetable garden. It was the first thing we needed, he said, and proceeded to prowl around, until he found the perfect spot beside the barn. This, he knew, was where all the manure had been pitched in past times. We dug where he suggested, and the vegetables have flourished ever since. Many unorthodox things slip in. The nets of pole beans are dotted with scarlet runner bean flowers, sown for hummingbirds; the patch of scarlet flowered bergamot intended to flavour our own Earl Grey tea also attracts the hummingbirds. By mid-July the whole thing will be a tangle of herbs and bees and birds and flowers, yet always the vegetables are enough for our year.

I'd like to tell you more about the garden, but it is the wildness here that is more important. Let's walk on through the park a little, and then we might go back together to Spy Rock. There we can sit here in the sun while the light is high and the views are good. Welcome. There's so much to talk about here.

Spring

The land that still has tall trees

"Do you know of any land in this area that still has tall trees?" I asked a conservation-minded friend. During the two years we had lived in eastern Ontario my husband Barry and I had looked often for a woods like the ones I remembered from childhood. What we wanted was a wood with trees leafy enough to cast a heavy shade in summer, with hollow old trunks to attract woodpeckers, a woods with a few trees broad enough to hide behind. To our disappointment what we had found so far were only thickets of wrist-thick, characterless saplings.

"You might try the conservation area near Westport," my friend suggested. "There's a large stand of big pine there – the same tall trees they used to cut for ship masts in the eighteen hundreds, actually. That's the only place I can think of. Everywhere else gets logged over pretty regularly. I hear the Conservation Authority is thinking of hiring a supervisor for the place next year, someone to look after it and teach a few classes," he added.

It wasn't until late afternoon on a March day too early for spring and too late for winter that we saw Foley Mountain for the first time. As yet unspoken was the real reason we had come to look at the park: if we liked it we might think of trying for the supervisor's job.

The pines of our search were bending under a raw wind as we approached the entrance gate to the park. In spite of the bleak day we felt at home seeing them. Because the road into the park was still crusted with snow and unrutted by cars, we decided to park at the gate and go in on foot. And so, for the first time, we set out along the road through the deep forest, trudging over the gritty snow and admiring the look of the white birches that grew among the huge pines.

At the first turn in the lonely road, we came upon a cleft where the melting snow had cut a broad channel in the softening earth of the road. No wonder no cars had been in before us. We forded the washout and continued until the dense woods ended and rough fields began. Over a hill some distance from the road we could see the small white farmhouse that would become the supervisor's residence. There was far more land here to explore than we had thought. Although we hadn't looked at the house yet, the road curved on ahead of us invitingly. We must come back soon and spend a day, we said, but for now we would just walk down to the bend in the road to see if we could get an idea of how far the park extended.

Crossing an open field now, the road was bare of snow and soft to our feet as we hurried down the slope to the curve. There we stopped in surprise. Ahead of us, the road plunged down a long, steep hill, but what caught our breath was the cascade that tumbled and pounded down the rocky hillside, shaking the ground beneath our feet.

I crouched beside the waterfall, letting the spray touch my face and watching the water's force tearing at loose rocks. "We've never seen anything like this," I exulted.

It's amazingly wild here," Barry said. "We're only a mile or so from Westport, but I doubt if many people have seen this."

The fading light told us that we would have to hurry back to the car, but as we were walking back Barry said, "I should phone the Authority about that washout," and as we got into the car he added, "The job here would certainly be worth seeing about."...

We've lived in the supervisor's house "up on the Mountain" for more than a dozen years, yet the pines still wave as alluringly as they did that first day and any time now the ice will shatter, releasing the waterfall once more.

The spirit of a countryman

He's gone now, the first friend we made when we moved to Westport, but when I remember Stan Crawford, I often am reminded that the influence of a person continues on after death like the rings from a stone cast into the lake.

At first when he died and I passed the snug white house at the foot of the hill I felt only saddened by his absence, sorry that we would no longer be friendly rivals in gardening matters nor share a keen delight in deer and their wiliness. Stan's life had been long, and until very near the end he had been able to enjoy what meant most to him, keeping in close touch with wildness. He'd had the happiness of living with his wife in a home dear to their heart, a home with many things he had made for it himself, and he'd had also the satisfaction of many good friends, and a just pride in many quietly performed kindnesses. There could be no regret for him, yet I felt his absence.

It was in late August of the summer Stan died that I found the wild honey bees in the woods a mile or so from his home. In all likelihood these bees had arrived as a swarm that had taken off in a cloud one fine summer morning from one of the old-fashioned hives at the back of Stan's garden. At that time his were the only hives in the area. How fitting it was, I thought, as I watched the bees foraging in the pale woodland goldenrod flowers, that some of his bees had moved to the woods he loved better than anything. The bees had taken flight and lived on now, in an independence that matched Stan's, helping to keep the forest flowers alive.

Stan had been the first visitor to welcome us when we moved to "the Mountain", inching along the snowy park road in his old blue car to give us an idea of how pleased he was that the land was now a park with a live-in supervisor to care for it. Bogged down in unpacking and adjusting to a new house, we regained our enthusiasm for the place while talking to Stan. Had we seen deer tracks near the house? He had come up to the park winter mornings and found groups of "lying down places" in the snow right by the house, right by it. It had been Stan's dream to see the big, pine-clad ridge behind his house preserved as a conservation area, a dream for which he had worked hard, and he couldn't tell us enough about its lore. Much of what he told us and taught us to watch for has found its way into Barry's classes and now travels home with people as diverse as schoolchildren from Westport who take pride in their past, and visitors who come from as far away as Prince Edward Island.

Later it was Stan who tramped out with us in mud-time to pick a site for our garden. Each time I look out over the beautiful, productive bed he chose for us, sheltered from the prevailing winds and nourished by the rich layer of sheep manure he knew had been piled there in earlier days, Stan is with us again, Stan and the earlier lovers of this land who gave it their care and understanding. For I often sense the influence of earlier settlers here as well. Whoever planted our small orchards had a fine appreciation of their needs, for instance. As for the man who planted the cottonwoods in front of our house, surely he knew how much the shade and shelter would be valued.

Others who are gone have left their mark on the area too, those whom I used to see come to the park to take in its solitude and give it their appreciation. These men and I never exchanged more than a quick glance as we moved to our own special places alone. I will not see them or Stan again, yet they are not gone from my thoughts as I watch a wood duck swim alone in the centre of the beaver pond or hear a loon's call rising from the mist, just as these things must have happened when they walked in the pinewoods. As surely as phosphorescence glows in the woods at night, I do believe that the spirit of a countryman lives beyond him in many ways.

Walking the dog

Barry and I have an ongoing wrangle about having our dog, Grog, along on walks. "Leave the dog at home," Barry insists. "He'll scare off every creature for miles around. You can bring him if you want, but you won't see anything."

I acknowledge the truth in what he says. A thundering, barking dog dashing around in circles is bound to scare off birds and animals, yet out of pity I often do let Grog come along, at least on walks of my own. The very haphazard chasing that Barry complains of sometimes works to my advantage too. For instance, without Grog, I wouldn't have know there were twenty-six ducks in a certain small pond near here.

Mind you, the word "accompaniment" would have to be taken loosely. I have yet to own a dog whose idea of a walk consisted of trotting sedately by my side. I suspect I wouldn't care much for such a dog anyway, no matter how likeable he might otherwise be. A typical excursion with Grog might include distant sightings of a black, brown and white streak rushing through the thick grass two fields away, and a splashing plunge as he flings himself into a fetid pond to cool off, followed by some bounding and shaking intended to encourage me to increase my pace. It also would include furtive jinglings of dog tags heard from the woods where he vainly hunts rabbits, and finally, a zigzagging canter over rockpiles where he seeks out groundhogs. This could hardly be called going for a walk *with* Grog.

Grog's walks are all the more passionate because he is confined half the year on account of the deer in the area. Even in winter, though, when I must take him on a leash, I find his enthusiasm adds to my experience. I like holding his leash because, if I'm attentive enough, I can sense more about my surroundings than I could on my own. Many times I would miss seeing a deer standing motionless in the forest if it weren't for the silent quiver of excitement that travels from Grog to me by way of the leash. There's no denying dogs are far from wild, yet their keen awareness and instinctive behaviour makes me realize how much we have forsaken of our past.

Walking with Grog I take pleasure in sharing his infectious enjoyment, but at times I also must take part in his other emotions. Above all I remember a moment of fear. One evening in early spring I set out with him for a brief walk down the road to the waterfall and back. As we walked, Grog pulling jauntily at his leash, a flurry of wet snowflakes whitened the road. Just at the top of the hill, Grog suddenly stopped dead and the fur on his back rose in the air, but to my surprise he did not challenge whatever had attracted his attention. His unusual fear was catching and, as I could see little in the blurring snow, I gave up on the waterfall and turned to go home. Before us on the snowy road, I saw footprints so large they looked like those of a barefooted man. When I checked a reference book at home, I learned Grog's fear had been of a bear newly out of hibernation, and I felt thankful I had not been alone to blunder on without warning.

There are times, likely quite a few of them, when a dog-less walk is to be preferred. But when I think of the joy of country life my thoughts always include a plucky fool of a dog bounding through forest and field, his ears streaming as he rushes off towards the sun.

Sap-boiling time

I got a letter from Susan the other day, a rare and happy occurrence because she does not like writing letters. This one came to me because she had been sitting boiling sap in her family's sugar house, and, over the long hours in the smoky shanty, she had been remembering when we were neighbours. Maple syrup making, coming as it does on the verge of spring, is one of the evocative times, and reading Susan's welcome letter brought back memories for me too.

What I remembered, thinking of Susan and syrup, was the year I brought my first baby home. I'd gone into the hospital in a snowstorm and two weeks later I returned to hear red-wings and rills of water running off the hilly fields. The sky seemed to open up before me with the very happiness of it all. In those days Susan and her brothers were all at school during the day and her Dad, for the first time, was working away from Blue Ridge Farm. The boys collected sap before they left each morning, but on days when the flow was heavy, it was spilling out of the buckets by noon. Glad of the experience, Barry walked up to the farm each day to help and came back to Morgan and me smelling, for the first time, of that sweetish spring smell of boiling sap. That fragrance, and the happiness that came with it, became then and afterwards a part of my spring.

Reading Susan's letter I thought that to know syrup-making time you have to live with it. No day visit to a demonstration bush will do. The time of the sap flow is, as Vermonters claim, a special extra season. As much as anything, making maple syrup provides a chance to live outside at this turning point between winter and spring. Just when the longing for spring becomes intolerable, along comes a special, once-a-year kind of work which says that spring is closer than you thought. Making syrup keeps you close to the pulse of spring.

When the ground is still stony hard and clouds close over, the sap drops cling to the spiles. Put your finger to a spile and it's hard to catch enough of the thin, sweetish drops for a test. Then one day sun floods the bush and the sap wells over. "There's a rush today. By Jeez, is she ever flowing today!" – and every spare woman, man and child is coaxed out to empty the pails and watch the fires. Before the first warm day ends snow seems to shrivel off the fields. At the one tricky hill on the way back to the shanty, the horse-drawn sleigh runners catch and drag through the mud and it's time to hitch up the wagon.

It begins to look like the days of the syrup flow could go on forever, and the syrup makers begin to think more of long nights stoking fires and staring into evaporator pans and less of how fine the harvest is. Woodpiles dwindle and weary backs begin to speak of "just one more bucket to throw up into the collecting wagon." The stickiness is no longer so sweet – now it's a mess that clings to your hair, and your clothes, a smell you can't shake sleeping or waking.

Then one night you step out to have a look at the moon and find your winter jacket is too heavy. The temperature isn't dropping the way it used to. In the light the shanty window throws, you see the first of the flittery "syrup moths" that appear late in the season. Next morning, stopping to rest, you look up into the maples and see that the buds have swelled almost to flowering. True spring has replaced sap season.

The force that through the green fuse

It was an acorn that started me thinking. I was walking along the rocky path of the Wildflower Trail when my toe raised an acorn. This was not one of the glossy, solid nuts of late autumn, though. This was an acorn that had felt Dylan Thomas' "force that through the green fuse drives the flower". For when I picked it up I found that the husk had softened and a shoot had thrust through its wooden case and reached out towards the soil. In my hand I held the makings of a tree. I looked at my feet and saw more riven acorns and shoots. I had come upon an oak nursery.

Now I heard a cat-like squalling and a scrambling in the trees overhead and I looked up. Powered by the same force that drove the root out of the acorn shell, no less than five kittenish squirrels dashed round and round through the surrounding trees. It was likely that some of the rubble that lay at my feet could be traced to their relatives. But someday even these acorn husks would serve to nourish the meagre soil of the forest floor.

I laid down my acorn and softened the fragrant forest earth around its shoot, hoping to make an easier passage for it. It was white oak territory here, and while I scratched in the rubble of shells and twigs I though of our deer and how the rich, oily acorns in fall provided them with fat layers to survive the winter.

About me everything from earth to air had the electric quickness of spring. The stream ahead of me tumbled over itself in a foaming rush to reach the lake. On both sides of the trail were a froth of wildflowers hurrying to fulfil their cycle. Soon the trees would leaf out and the forest canopy would close off their light.

But after seeing the acorn nursery I was thinking of seeds. In the woods, if I looked closely, there were seeds in a wild generosity. It was this abundance of possibility that fascinated me.

I thought first of the winged seeds, the maple keys beloved of children. Whirled by a rudder, on severing from its tree, each pair of seeds floated down to spread upon the ground. Dandelion and goatsbeard travelled far with their parachutes. Perhaps loveliest of all seed dispersals was a field dreamy with milkweed down after the weathered grey pods had split open. Even deep in the woods I sometimes found a seed and its carrier, wind-driven into an unlikely landing bed.

Then there were the fruit-encased seeds. Near me I saw the rounded twin leaves of clintonia and reminded myself to look for the indigo berries this fall. I passed the nondescript flower of white baneberry, remembering its large white berries like china dolls' eyes in the fall. Against a log I found a wintergreen plant with one remaining, bright red berry. I slit it open with my thumbnail and looked at the tiny seeds before I ate it. Back on the rocky path I saw the flowers of the woods strawberry and thought of its berries with seeds sunk in little pits on the outside. There are so many variations on the theme, each subtly adapted to its individual need to repeat itself.

I passed the hollow where there is a stand of cockleburs in fall. Burrs must be one of the least likeable methods of transference of seeds. Still, these seeds travel as effectively as those that fly or appeal to taste.

Last of all, across the bridge I came to a solitary pine, out of place in a forest where hardwoods predominate. For the pine, the cone is the seeds' case in a complicated process that can sometimes take two years to complete. Hidden within the cone seeds and wings develop to be spread, sometimes by the same squirrels who shift acorns.

With my thoughts back to the acorns again, it occurred to me that seeds fascinated me because they are at the pivotal point between what has been and what will be. Around me I can, at the same time, see wildflowers hurrying to end their cycles by producing seeds and an acorn (the seed itself) thrusting forth to begin its cycle.

Elegy for a place that is lost

This is an elegy for a place that is dead. Even as I write, the bulldozers are moving in. A few people understand how land can grow inside your heart until it's as much a part of your blood as your family, but many don't. For those who also have a lost woods I am writing this.

When I think of it now, I realize the place was dying even while I was growing up and losing my heart to it. On wild March nights I lay awake hearing the rending of trees and in the morning I went out to find new victims felled. The chain of reasons why my place, my home, was falling apart are complex, but it always came down to the encroachment of people.

At first there was an old orchard along the woods' margin, an orchard of gnarled trees and knee-long grass. In spring on steamy hot days I used to slip out of the woods to look at the foamy blossoms and copper-coloured bark. Often I heard the cock pheasant honking for his hen or saw him pacing among the spilling petals.

Then the tangled beauty was gone. Where branches had arched were brick boxes and flat squares of mowed grass. Where there had been grassy lanes there was now asphalt, each driveway being decorated with two or three splashy cars and a big boat. The pheasant and I withdrew into the woods. Still there was the woods.

But now the trees kept falling. As my father explained it to me, opening up the subdivision had exposed the edge of the woods to wind and sunlight that they were not equipped to tolerate. Roots had been damaged too. The effect was like toppling a house of cards. As each row fell, another row was opened up to be attacked.

As things happened in this chain, there was a stream, a sparkling, meandering Tennyson's Brook of a stream that cut through the heart of our property. Other housing developments were built farther up the stream and I began to know washing day by the soap suds floating through our woods. Other days the stream turned an evil and unexplained red. Now in storms trees were wrenched up by their roots in the heart of the woods as well as at the edge. came to see that for the beloved forest, there was no hope of healing because new saplings had stopped springing up. Was it because of the emissions from the factories down by the lake as well as the poisoned water and soil?

As the little place shrank in on itself, the animals and birds increased, driven there by the diminishing shelter in our neighbourhood. One spring morning my father and I counted fifty species of migrant birds. Foxes, absent for thirty years, reappeared, and, most wonderful of all, at daybreak my father saw a fawn poised under the beeches. Where are they all now that the last refuge is gone?

When I first learned the place was condemned I felt the white-hot pain of loss. It was unthinkable that I could never return and that, worse still, the woods was to die.

But, after all, I do see it still. Even as the last trees shake the ground and the hummocks and hollows are levelled, I see instead a little girl dressed in red hunched beneath a hemlock fingering its cones like rosary beads and listening to a kind rain touching the leaves on the ground around her. The girl grows older but the woods still sustains her and now she sits reading in a hammock stretched between two beeches, stroking the glassy pleats of their new leaves. Still later, the girl clings to an old vine-hung tree that reaches out over a pond and looks out at the world. Always for her the world was seen through a frame of leaves. And then it is autumn and, home from school, she stands alone among an anthem of leaves playing the fiddle, playing for the one audience that always approves, the leaves bursting, floating, and falling like waves around her, endless. Ended.

"Where did you go?" "Out."

It's been a "Where did you go?" "Out." "What did you do?" "Nothing." kind of day. I didn't quite skip when I started down the lane this morning after the boys left on the school bus, but I did splash through three puddles and scrunch the icy edges of a fourth as I sallied out "just because". I'm happy to say I even managed not to look around to see if anyone was watching.

Behind me I left assorted unfinished work piled on my desk in the trailer, (I bounced a handful of gravel over the still-frozen pond beside the road) and in the house my house-keeping was even less worthy than usual. (With a stick I scratched deliberately in the frost-crinkled mud at my feet). For all that the early morning wind was still cold, I tore off my hat and let the wind take my hair. When I reached the top of the hill a recently-returned crow blew past me. I thrust up my arms to him and I could almost sense approval in the caws that came back to me on the wind.

Most of my friends are very grown up indeed, and, I'm sorry to say, even many of the kids I know look and sound like little old men and women. Somehow I don't fit in. I am still asking myself "What are you going to be when you grow up?" and I suspect that the answer is always going to be "I don't know", because I can't imagine arriving at that sober and rigid state.

When I was four, I remember, I cried over a song about childhood: "Once you reach its borders you can never go back again," it said. Even then I was sure that being condemned forever to adulthood would be an awful fate. As I've watched friends succumb I've realized being grown up means being careful not to care too much. It means, in fact, being careful in general, rather than playful, and it was here that I drew the line this breezy spring morning. As I kicked a stone along the road I thought that the words of the song didn't need to come true. The best things about childhood: wonder, fantasy, enthusiasm, intensity of vision and playfulness are with us always. It's just that most people let themselves lose touch with them.

Farther down the road I saw a mourning cloak butterfly fanning on a rotten log, the first I'd seen out of hibernation. I squatted beside it to look at it more closely. (Taking time to look deeply like thirsty drinking is one of the delights of an "I'm just going out – nowhere special" kind of day.) Crouched in the warming sun with the wind in the bare branches overhead, the wine-coloured butterfly and the earthy scent of the log was so heady that it all became too much for me and I jumped up and continued on.

Over the next hill I came upon a most satisfying sight. A still-frozen culvert had caused a large puddle to spread across the road. The responsible adult in me knew I could and should deal with this to prevent the possibility of bone-jolting bumps and wash-outs. But what most adults wouldn't admit as they scraped and dug a series of channels, is how good the mud feels beneath the boot heel and how delicious it is to watch the water creep then rush from the puddle until the road is clear again.

With my road-work completed, I headed for the open field where the high March wind reminded me of kites. At first I thought of waiting for the boys to come home from school. Already I could feel the wind calling the paper bird higher, though. I didn't need the rationale of children to justify capering wildly across the field.

I went home to dig out the boys' kite and that ball of kite string I had seen down behind the toy chest. All afternoon I "wasted" my time with the kite. But what about you? When was the last time you laughed yourself silly just for the sheer fun of laughing, played with the kids' finger paints without considering the mess, rolled over the way a lion would, just to see what it feels like?

25

There's a wake in town tonight

Passing the local furniture store cum funeral parlour at dusk I see there's to be a wake later on. The white curtains are closed over the display window, shutting out the furniture aspect of the business. As always, I feel a shiver of anxiety and regret. What familiar face is gone now? Who has our community lost?

In all the weeks of the past long, cold winter, I reflect, scarcely one has passed without a death relevant to our rural area. Each week, it seems, new mourners have been gathered at the store.

Although the day had been warm, it is still early enough in spring that the temperature drops severely when the sun sets. In the last cool clear light a robin warbles among the swelling maple flowers, but the ice has not yet gone from the lake.

Some of the wakes, particularly those for the very old who have outlived their families, have had only a few watchers, but in this case the cars already exceed the available space and crowd both sides of the street.

In the half-light I can see into the lit parlour from the opening door. I see stiff men standing awkwardly, helplessly, in seldom-used suits, and can imagine the hectic warmth and the sense of unreality within the crowded room.

Standing apart as I am in the cool evening, watching nameless people mourn a nameless death, I think how hard it would be to die now, at the season's turning. All winter I had watched the village aged, hunched over against icy winds, making their way in measured steps, slowly along the slippery sidewalks. To die now, as all that was ending… And yet, I asked myself, at what season would you choose to die?

Because it is men who are bunched near the door, I conjecture that it was a man who had died and that the women are inside close to his widow. I see on the men's faces not tragedy, but an expected death, I imagine her loneliness, and think of the hard new road ahead for her with a chill that does not come from the ice on the nearby lake.

Because there are many pick-up trucks among the vehicles in the parking lot I surmise that the dead man was a farmer. At a farm nearby it may be that, for the first time, this year the fields will go unploughed, as they are now at so many of the farms hereabouts. When the killdeers return, there will be no freshly turned earth to greet them.

I am expected at home and must leave now. The old at the wake may linger a little, may remember the dead with kindness, perhaps with amusement. And out of this they will draw a little closer in the coming night. They will listen to each other with keener ears, delighting in those who are left, pleased that there is someone left who remembers, still someone who knows just how strong John used to be and what a fine lot of work he could do. There may yet be someone who can say, "Oh, I used to see your father do that exactly the same way." Only in that gathering can yesterday and the dead one of the wake truly be celebrated.

Outside the funeral parlour, while I have stood apart watching, the darkness has been made complete, and I lay down my thoughts, the only wreath I can offer, and turn away towards home.

A kind of pearly grey day

There's a kind of pearly grey day in spring that brings a restlessness that is hard to deal with. On such a day, staying indoors and settling down to work is out of the question. Even in the woods I find myself moving aimlessly, disturbed by the queer, ashen light that comes through bare trees when their leaf buds are on the point of opening. Under my feet the light is echoed by the dead leaves and skeletons of leaves that I tread on, leaves that have been matted by the winter's weight of snow. On this windless day, the woods is perfectly still and the only sound is the monotonous shrill of the peepers.

In front of me, most precious because she is a herald of all the butterflies to come, flits a mourning cloak butterfly, the first of the year, and at last my attention is caught. The cream-bordered, wine-coloured butterfly is the first touch of brightness that I have come upon in the woods, and I follow her wavering flight with interest as she passes from leaf to leaf with movements as vague as today's light.

The pale sun has sent a weak shaft of light through the clouds to make a warm patch on the leaves of the forest floor, where the mourning cloak lands, and I sit down on the wooden bridge that spans the stream to watch her fan her wings: closed they are indistinguishable from the dead leaves on which she rests, fanned open to accept the sun, their dusky maroon lining glows. I look at the butterfly, so perfectly shaped, and consider afresh how she hibernates over winter. I have never been lucky enough to actually see her slip under bark in fall or emerge in spring, and I cannot imagine how in her papery delicacy she manages it.

The sun cannot last on this day of pervasive cloud, and when it retreats, the butterfly moves on, leaving me to look more deeply at my surroundings. I realize now that the restlessness the day called forth at first was not the right response. As I become perfectly still, absorbed in the butterfly, the woods, which had seemed eery and unapproachable to me, begins to open up and give me images of unusual beauty.

On both sides of the stream I notice that the mottled leaves of dogtooth violets have pushed up everywhere through the dead forest floor. In their urgency, they have even pierced some of the toughest of all the dead leaves. Close to the sheltering warmth of a large rock, I see arching yellow sprays of bellwort, and then, looking more closely, I see that the ground is really a tapestry of flowers so pale and delicate that at first I had missed them. Certainly they had not been blooming when I had passed this way less than a week ago. The slight pink of spring beauty, the fringed leaves and pantaloon-shaped flowers of Dutchman's breeches, and the starry foam flower – the more intensely I look at the covering of dead leaves, the more it comes alive with flowers.

Occasionally, beige "sugar moths", so named because of their appearance at the same time that maple syrup making is waning, drift like spirits over the blossoms.

But now the clouds are getting denser, and, with the coming of a new chill to the air, I am reminded of the work waiting at home, and start back across the bridge. On the homeward side of the stream stands a silvery beech, an aged crone of a beech, bent and gnarled.

About her grows a dense thicket of infant beeches. Still looking for wildflowers, I find a great cluster of hepaticas tucked among the young trees, their downy stems and new leaves complimenting the greyness of the beeches, and kneel down to savour the rose and mauve flowers.

When I entered the grey woods a few hours ago, I had felt at odds with myself and the woods, yet, through the grace of an early butterfly and a host of frail flowers, I leave in peace.

The lottery

When our boys came home from school muttering about a lottery for Easter and winning a real, live rabbit, we tried to close our ears. "If you win," I said, "you just will have to put the ticket back in the pot for some other kid. Where would we keep a rabbit? And anyway, there are too many animals in this house already. I don't know why the two of your bother," I added. "You know we never win anything. McQuays aren't lucky."

I should have known by the look on Morgan's face that he wouldn't give up that easily. Every day of the week before Easter the boys came home with fresh news of the rabbit. "I got to hold her today, Mommy," announced Jeremy.

"Her fur is really soft, isn't it, Jeremy," said Morgan, "but aren't her claws sharp? If she doesn't want you to hold her she kicks and scratches like mad."

"Did you get your tickets yet?" I asked, purely out of form, and they nodded firmly. What I didn't know was that in his determination to win, Morgan had taken three dollars of saved-up allowance to buy tickets with which to stuff the lottery box.

The Thursday afternoon before Good Friday I was hurrying to finish my writing for the week when the phone rang. "Mommy," a small voice said, "It's Morgan. You'll never guess what."

"What?" I asked absent-mindedly, calculating whether there would be time to get him to the doctor if he was phoning home sick.

"I won the rabbit, and Mrs. Blair says could you please bring a box when you come over to pick us up. I don't think the rabbit would like to ride on the school bus."

"I thought this wasn't going to happen," I suggested to Morgan. "Well, I have to go now," he evaded. "Don't forget the box."

I should have been mad. I should have been worried. What would Barry say? Where would we put the creature? Heavens, tomorrow was Good Friday and the lumberyard would be closed. I wouldn't even be able to build the wretched thing a cage. "McQuays never win anything," I said to myself. I found a large cardboard box and started the car. Beyond carrots I didn't even know what pet rabbits eat.

I arrived at the school prepared to put my foot down. We just couldn't have another pet and Morgan knew that as well as I did. Some other child would have to take that rabbit. It was impossible. I had forgotten the infectious exuberance of a school full of kids and teachers about to be released for the first long weekend of spring. As I entered the hall full of milling kids, laughing and shrieking, Jeremy's teacher came up to me.

"You should have seen Jeremy when Morgan's name was picked," she said. "He jumped way up in the air and I don't think his feet have hit the floor yet. I've never seen a kid so excited."

A passing boy said, "Yeah, and you should have seen Morgan when the photographer took his picture with the rabbit for the paper. Is he ever lucky."

From the dark at the end of the hall I could hear a chorus of "Let me see. Let me see" and soon Morgan was standing before me, holding a box with a cowering grey Easter rabbit. He looked at me with shining eyes and we both looked at the rabbit, while Jeremy and his friends capered around us.

After a long moment I said, "Well, I suppose we'd better get it home before it dies of fright."

When we arrived home the rabbit would have to learn to live with our dog, who, up to now had looked on rabbits as victims, and three cats who preferred not to deal with strangers of any kind. I thought of our rabbit-height, plant-filled window sills and sighed. For now, though, it was the beginning of Easter and two joyous, small boys and a grey rabbit were walking out into the sunlight.

A time apart

It seems right with things trembling on the verge of spring to set aside a day to be clear of food and everyday preoccupations. For me it has become a day to walk lightly from the house and roam the fields and woods, searching for spring, exulting in solitude.

And so, at noon I wander freely across the sodden fields, unsure of what direction to take and caring little. Time is long. I can spill it through my hands like beach sand. The only clock I follow is the arc of a wan sun. All morning the newly-returned red-winged black-birds have carolled, but now, in early afternoon, all bird song has stopped. In this great, sere field I hear only water rilling everywhere. Here I find the bleached, grassy tangle of a mouse nest. All winter it has lain beneath a snow drift. Now it lies here flattened and exposed to me and the fitful wind.

A little lightheaded for want of food I wander, gazing at the sky and the shifting clouds that subdue the sun, until I stumble over a spring, the source of a stream which crosses the lowest ground of the field. I am delighted to see it because it bubbles out of a cleft in a rock pile for only a few weeks. The years I look for it I cannot find it. Only if I stumble over it will it reveal itself. For a few minutes I forget the insistence of my hunger and stand fascinated by the clear water stirring the long-dead field grasses. Within its clarity I see the tiny, verdant leaves of cinquefoil waving in the water at the spring's base. It is a first sign of the greening of a new season that appears in the grey and snow-beaten field.

From the spring I loiter along the stream bed to a place which green has not touched yet. In the oak woods I come to a world closed in, where last year's leaves still hang on the trees, leathery and crisp. A cloud hides the sun and out of the gray stillness comes a fit-ful breeze. I hear the whirring, feathered flight of a woodpecker and search him out. The red splash on his head is the only touch of col-our in this whispering dead world. The woodpecker is the only vital thing in this place of grey, shaggy trees and faded leaves, and I lean against a tree to watch him.

Again the pale sun appears, and, in its slight warmth I fall into a hungered daze, not caring if I move on or spend the afternoon in the woods. Here everything seems suspended, yet there is new life. Six recently returned crows flapping by with ragged, fingered wings arouse me. The sun is much lower now, and its new slant lights the crows' waxy feathers as they pass. I remember that I had wanted to move on to the beaver pond today. As I leave the oak woods I see patches of grainy snow in the clefts of rocks, and then, in the shelter of a rock I find the last year's leaves of a hepatica and pull them gently apart to find the furry, silky new stems and curled fists of buds.

To get to the pond I follow a grove of young aspens down the slope to the water. This is always a place of early greenness. Just now the pointed aspen buds are sticky and swollen, and I see a grouse feeding high in a spindly tree. Illuminated by the red sun the bird looks like a medieval tapestry of a partridge in a pear tree. From the aspen grove I go down the beaver drag to the pond and lean against a red maple. Here I scan the open water for early ducks.

The sun is once more behind a cloud, but I can see that the pond is right on the verge of change. Down by the far curve rotten ice still holds the shore, but where I stand, close to the dam, the wind riffles the open water ever so slightly and then subsides to let the surface become a black mirror for the tangle of still-bare tree branches.

No ducks are here yet, but there are signs that the beaver have been out. There is much fresh cutting. The dam is fortified with new sticks, and sap bleeds from the wounds that beaver teeth have given to the maple that I lean against.

By now the light is so dim in the woods that I will need to be careful making my way home. My stomach no longer pangs, but I am giddy. My day is all but accomplished, and, with the tree silhouettes of maple flowers against the red-stained sky, it is time to let myself think of the joys ahead. Leaves will follow the maple flowers, and oh, to hear a wind in the leaves again! A heron will stand at the neck of his pond before long. Soon insects will quicken the air over the pond, not altogether a cheering thought, but with their arrival will come swallows, forked and winged. My new lightness has nothing to do with an empty stomach.

As I move towards the fields and home, clouds are taking the red from the sky and bringing a promise of rain, a rain that overnight will draw green shoots through the dead field grass.

The death of a deer

It was on the Saturday between Good Friday and Easter that I saw him. I was just beginning to work on the three braids of the special bread I always make for Easter. As I rolled out the dough I listened to the liquid song of the red-winged blackbirds through windows open for the first time since they were sealed last fall. I heard the blackbirds' song and enjoyed it, but my mind was still lingering on Good Friday as I reworked old and hopeless thoughts of how cruelty and injustice flourish as greenly as ever around the world. My fingers formed the braids and secured them, and I brushed the egg mixture gently over the beautiful loaf, but I scarcely knew what I was doing. Absent-mindedly I tucked the bread away for a last rising and glanced out the window over the rocks. And there he stood, a large deer poised on the granite not five feet from my window.

Slowly, carefully, I knelt on the couch in front of the window, staring in disbelief and delight at a deer who would approach so close to our house in the broad morning light. Often deer came around, but generally by stealth and at night. Also, I knew many of the deer had already left the park for the lonelier places where they would summer.

And still he held his ground, his coat greyed with its winter tones, but velvet and glowing against the mist rising off the fields. Perhaps he had come to visit the compost pile as the night visitors do, I thought. But why did he just stand quivering and staring at me, so close to the house? Most deer I encountered at such a distance would have given me a sound stamp and strode or leapt away from me.

I leaned forward on the couch, beginning to realize that there was something wrong with the trembling stillness I was seeing. This was a deer that was lean but yet not as gaunt as some I have watched. It could not be that he was starving, surely. Then a car went by on the road and he jerked his head and moved as slowly as a ghost off in the direction of the barn. As I saw the gait of this shadowy deer, I felt tugged by a gust of pity and awe and something more. Almost before my eyes, as he drifted over the lawn, he was fading. I was in on a death.

Everywhere around me the red-wings carolled. The sun that came in the window was warm and full of strength. Somewhere nearby in the woods a grouse was drumming with vitality. Oh life: to survive winter and leave in spring. I stared at the deer, who was too numb even to be aware of the force I put into my look, urging him to revive. And still he moved on with unspeakable grace, with a queer certainty, until his grey-gold blended with the faded grass of the field and he was gone from my sight.

Always there's the longing to make things come right in the end. I sorted through my possibilities: perhaps the fine days ahead would restore him; I could place a pile of special food out on the granite; if all else failed, should there not be a bullet to end…? I was still staring off across the field so fixedly that the withered grasses were beginning to dance and mingle before my eyes. By what right did I think to intervene? In the tree outside the window the red-wings' song was strong with life and so was beautiful. But, I had to ask myself, was there anything less compelling, less right, about the slow dignity of the failing deer?

Tree planting

With a spade, a pail of water, some barren-looking twigs of trees and a proper following of children and dogs, we set off over the field one light spring evening to begin our annual spring tree planting.

Given all the busyness that spring demands, our tree-planting ceremonies are apt to be haphazard. "How many trees did you say were in the bundle that came today?" Barry will ask wearily when he comes in for his supper after dealing with fifty bouncy school children all day. And indeed, what seemed a fine vision of larches, spicebush, mountain ash, russian olives and dogwood in January becomes a more serious proposition when a burlap sack arrives demanding twenty carefully dug holes in well-chosen sites on an acutely busy day.

Before I came to Foley Mountain I never lived anywhere longer than a year and a half, and consequently I have left a trail of trees behind me in selected sites all over Ontario, rather like lesser Johnny Appleseed. To many people, tree-planting on rented property is a wasteful idea, and it is true that to this day I have never been able to look upwards at any tree I have planted, yet every spring, as the earth quickens, I know that nothing is more of an affirmation of faith in the world than planting a tree.

I've learned a lot since the first trees I planted. I think at last I've outgrown my beginner's tendency to place trees too close together. At first it was hard to believe that the slender, knee-high saplings I put in would, in the days of my children, reach eighty feet high and shade a whole lawn. Watching locusts I've planted in the Conservation Area grow to lock thorns at the age of three, I've had to learn to be more realistic in my spacing.

Since the second spring for my pear trees, when I found them standing lifeless in pools of water, I've become much more appreciative of good drainage. I've learned to study the location of the old local orchards common to this area. The qualities of site that have made them survive can be used to my advantage too.

Another problem to which I've become sensitive is prevailing winds. This spring I'll set out another witch hazel to replace the one that died last year, blasted by our northwest winter wind. This time I'll try to make a more temperate micro-climate for it by placing it in the shelter of a thicket of black cherries. I miss the fresh, wild scent of witch hazel flowers in October, and am not willing yet to acknowledge they are too tender for our area.

As trees are shaped by a wind, I've had to bend to accept the hard realities of my location with its worn-out, rocky soil and harsh climate, but I've never lost my delight in restoring trees to the land. In spite of my tiredness, the act of firming a small tree to stand upward in the ground is heartening, I think, as I form the rear of our straggling party, heading out now to plant this year's choicest tree, a chestnut.

One gloomy November day a year and a half ago, a friend dropped by with a bag of nuts from her city tree, saying perhaps our deer would enjoy them. I tucked a couple into the cold, wet soil, "just to see", never having experienced before the headiness of starting a tree from seed. Over the winter I forgot the glossy nuts, but next spring I noticed a sturdy shoot. We nursed it through a year, and now it was to grow on the hillside near the woods, to be within easy reach of any wildlife from the woods that might enjoy it.

Barry's spade cuts keenly, rending the dense sod of the field to expose fine, loose soil. The boys tip in their bucket of water and watch with pleasure as it oozes in. Then I stand holding the little tree lightly and watching the bright sun go down behind the hill. To plant a tree is to set dreams in motion, dreams of roots holding precious soil against erosion, of a plenitude of birds and animals, of shade and shelter, and ease for the eyes. It is living as if your tomorrow could last forever.

The flowery woods

There's not a minute to lose this time of year. In a single day's burst of heat a bloodroot's petals unfurl, spread, stretch and spill upon the ground. Wait only three days for the right time and you may miss that most fleeting of spectacles, the flowering of the trees.

I think it was living with our doorstep cottonwood trees that first made me think about the blooming of trees. Almost while I watch, the largest of the sticky, pointed buds splits and out falls a caterpillar – at least that is what the fat catkins bring to mind. In the slowest of motion, the tree becomes hung with catkins. Each day they lengthen until the cottonwood sways and dances with the Chinese red streamers. A little flock of brilliant yellow evening grosbeaks, absent in the month since our bird feeder was stored away. After just one more day, the pollen-heavy catkins slip from the two trees and clog the grass beneath them. The brief interlude of surprising beauty is at an end.

Walking out in search of blossoms I find the earliest of the blooms, the pussy willows, heavy with pollen. As our bees crawl back to the hives, baskets weighted with dust of many shades of green and gold, I realize all over again how much variety there is even in the mass of willows.

Next I look for the maples. If there were no other tree flower than these, the swamps and forests would be places of exceptional loveliness at this time. Even if I could not appreciate the crimson stars of their flowers myself, I would look at them just to catch a glimpse of squirrels in ecstasy, clinging perilously to the slightest of branches to taste the sweetness of the nectar within. Sometimes as I stand looking at the squirrels and the flowers, a rain of flower-ended twigs rattles down upon me.

Now, everywhere I go I see flowers. For just a few days, the blossoms of shadbush flicker through the woods like white flames. I angle around as manipulatively as a camera enthusiast posing a subject, until I stand where a shadbush throws its reflection onto the surface of a black little pool. No matter how hard I clutch at the image and try to fix it in my memory, I know that it will never have the richness of now.

In a clearing I find a honeysuckle, hung with twin bells and courted by bumblebees. I put out a finger and stroke the soft back of one delirious bee who is clinging to one of the bells so fiercely that he barely notices my intrusion.

Along the edge of the woods are Manitoba maples. At first these were some of the few trees I didn't appreciate. Brittle and weedlike, they usually could be found in tired soil by abandoned houses and roadsides. The slight, wispy flowers cannot hold a candle to alder catkins or swamp maple blooms, but I've come to value the trees now: the keys that drop from them each fall feed flocks of birds.

Last spring I looked across our fields to the pine forest west of us. For several days the air had been warm and still. Then, in late afternoon, a wind came up. As I looked, a yellow veil drifted down over the field, swirling and eddying. Was it dust from the road? Surely the earth was not that dry, and anyhow I could see that the dust was not coming from the road but from the pines. I realized that I was seeing something rare. The cloud was a rain of pine pollen released all at once by the sudden wind.

Although we may no longer be attuned to notice it when we enter the flowery woods, European explorer Arthur Barlowe has left us with a striking picture of how the woods' fragrance appeared to a sailor in 1584, "…we found shole water when we smelt so sweet and strong a smel, as if we had bene in the midst of some delicate garden abounding with all kinde of odiferous flowers, by which we were assured that the land could not be farre distant…"

The coil of things

The coil of things. The tangled and twisted beauty of the spiral, compressed and full of power. On a sunny morning I am picking my way over the rocks, unshaded by the as-yet-bare-branched oaks, looking for one of my favourite coils, that of newly emerged garter snakes. I've measured the day's warmth by the sun's touch on the back of my neck and, by my reckoning, this is a day to draw snakes from their rocky dens.

As I prowl over the rocks searching for the first snakes of spring, I look at lesser coils, admiring the ancient pattern of the spiral and its repetition throughout the woods. I look too, to see what life these spirals bind within them.

First to catch my attention is the hairy wild grape vine that loops and twists its way up and around a tree. At one point its grasp is so fierce that it has married with a branch of the tree, forcing a deep welt in the host's branch.

Then I notice the tight curls of ferns in a wet spot. From the spidery delicacy of the red royal fern to the tight-fisted thrust of the ostrich fern, each is wound tight as a spring and is also as poised as a spring. Within a week or two, as heat lures them on, the promise within the curve will burst out to feather the woods of summer.

As if tossed casually by an impersonal hand into a crevice, I see another spiral, the former home of a snail, now bleached chalk white. Land snails and water snails, from the tiniest pinheads of shells to the fist-sized shells of moon snails – each twisted home for its owner bears the same form, flaring at its exit, circling to a point at its core. Around this common, thumbnail-sized shell lie fragments of others. On the rocks are chambers, curves within curves. One shell is reduced to the skeleton of a spiral, an airy scaffold still pivoting on an axis.

I move on from the snail shells, looking for a flicker of green that will lead me to a snake, a garter snake, this commonest of snakes that I most wish to see in the design of the woods today. If ever the rocks and oaks seem sparse to me during the warm months, the motion of this striped snake enlivens them. Last November I saw the last few forced into lethargy by the cold. Now, with the sun's new strength, I hope for them again. My first snake, I miss. Tipping my way over uneven rocks, I see a head with unblinking eyes dart from a crevice. The snake sees me and races into a hole between rocks that I would never have noticed. I bend and peer into the hole where I can see the brightness of snake eyes. Over how many secret pools of life do I tramp in a day's walk?

My search goes on. What I find is much more than what I ex-pected. In the end it is sound that tips me off. A rustling of fallen oak leaves on a windless day draws me to a shallow ditch and there I see what I have never seen before, a writhing gathering of garter snakes tangled together to mate. Not one snake moved among the leaves but six, eight, ten. What called the snakes together: scent, vibrations? To a human watcher it appears wonderfully mysterious, this silent certainty of snakes fixed in their purpose. As I look, half of them, in-tent on their dance, slip down the ditch away from the main group. Labouriously, for it is still nowhere near a snake's preferred tempera-ture, they loop and drag their way back up the ditch's mountain.

Out of the sinewy spiral will come many new lives. The eggs will grow within the females, and still within, will hatch into snakelets which, unlike many snake young, will be born alive.

Cast a stone to see its rings; search out a spiral and see what is en-compassed. I leave the snakes in their revolving circle, brewing new life, and travel home.

The predator, not the prey

"Keer, keer, keer." The red-tails are back. The wild, free call rings in my ears and I search the sky for my first spring sighting of these large hawks. Yes, there is one, and, yes, a second, gliding dizzyingly high over the pasture. I watch them take the thermals and my heart soars too. I hear the piercing call again and I know that of all the returns this spring it is the hawks' that counts for most with me.

But it wasn't always this way. It took me a long time to appreciate raptors. My first memory of hawks is one of fear. One stony grey March day I was playing in the woods where I grew up when I felt a stare upon me. Never before or since have I sensed I was in the presence of such harshness. Although I wanted to run, something forced me to stay and I felt my eyes drawn up among the bare branches until I saw a large, dark bird and met his fierce, yellow eyes. At the time I was only seven or eight and I had never thought of the woods as other than friendly. I'd been reared on Thornton Burgess, Grey Owl and Beatrix Potter. In my place of "smiling pools" and "laughing brooks" the "good" animals always achieved "the dear old briar patch" in time.

This stranger was outside my knowledge and I was afraid. He made no sound; he didn't need to. I was gripped by his stare. I felt sick with a fear I'd never met before. How long I would have stayed mesmerized, I don't know, but my father came to see what I was looking at (if that paralysis could be called looking) and the hawk beat off through the branches. While I had been caught in the hawk's stare I'd realized that my play place was also his woods on his terms. Remembering the malevolence I'd sensed, I came to see the hawk and his brothers as dangerous and cruel intruders. My woods was never quite the same again.

It was three or four years later when I heard screams such as I had never dreamed of. I plunged through the snowy woods following the nightmare sounds to a clearing. Although the dreadful noise was out of my experience, I had no doubt that what I heard were mortal screams and I pushed my lungs to the burning point trying to intervene. The victim must be saved.

But I was too late. I did drive the large bird off the torn and bleeding cottontail, despite the frightful screams echoing in my head. But the rabbit, dear and soft and, in my mind, innocent, was dead now and I could not forgive the villain that had torn his life from him.

Not once did I stop to consider the bird. I didn't think that winter, when so much of his food hibernates, migrates, or goes beneath snow is as "cruel" to him as to the rabbit. It would not have occurred to me that my intervention had put the bird closer to the edge of starvation. I would not have thought rationally of the rabbit, either. Possibly sick or unfit, the swift, just end may well have been more merciful than the prolonged life I wished for it. It took me a long time to learn to respect a law that has no fairness in terms of sentiment, but is endlessly fair in the preservation of life itself.

Now, when I hear the "keer, keer," I look up with joy, for I've learned how wrong I was to assign good and bad roles in nature. All nature acting within its laws is to be respected equally. In some ways the predators are among the keepers of the laws. By their necessary diligence, only the soundest of the prey survive. Natural equilibrium is safeguarded. What I thought I saw as I bent and touched the rabbit's blood was cruelty. What I see now when I lift my head and exult with the free soaring hawks is a justice that restores the balance to the land I love. I feel as thankful for the hawk as for a cleansing wind that pares the land to beauty.

A little night music

"Not me," said our friend Jim, shaking his head as he loaded his suitcases into the trunk of his Volkswagen. "It was a great weekend, but I don't know how the two of you stand being so isolated out here." He looked around at our open fields, "It's all that quiet that's the hardest to take, especially at night. You just can't get a good night's sleep out here without any background noises to lull you off." He got into his car and waved at the boys. "You kids make sure your Mom and Dad bring you to Toronto some time soon so I can show you a really good time."

I shook my head as he drove away, and recalled what Beatrix Potter says at the end of *Johnny Townmouse*: "One place suits one person, another place suits another. For my part I prefer to live in the country."

How anyone can complain of quiet in the midst of the abundant sounds of our spring amazes me. After a long winter with windows taped shut against the cold I had been rejoicing in the night music that entered our newly opened bedroom window. In fact, I was almost at the point where I didn't want to waste time sleeping, the sounds of spring seemed so lovely to me.

The night Jim went back to Toronto, I sat at the window listening. As the sun set and the day's breeze died, all birdsong quieted even to the last liquid call of a redwing blackbird in the nearby pond. The sky paled, dusk advanced, and the scene was set for the fullness of the night.

The chorus began with the evening flight sounds of the newly returned woodcock. By day the plump, brown woodcock is a bird of the earth who spends his time digging worms out of wet areas with his absurdly long beak. But on spring nights he rises high in the air and then dives downwards making a metallic mating call. To hear the wild quavering of this clumsy, earthbound bird is, as naturalist Edwin Teale says, "one of the most profoundly moving events in the life of our meadows."

In the small pond at the bottom of our laneway ducks were quacking intimately together, in voices very different from their daytime exuberant chatter. Could these be the teals of last year, returned to raise more babies, or were they only migrants, stopping off on a flight to the north? As the sky darkened and the duck calls tapered off, the night chorus began with the throbbing of the peepers, mixed with the vigorous croaking of bullfrogs.

The night was full of life now. The moon was rising and I heard a fox bark in the woods. Close under my window the first call of a whippoorwill startled me with its loudness. Other whippoorwills answered his challenge until the field echoed with "whip-poor-will, whip-poor-will." How could anyone call a night with such resonant sounds quiet?

By simply following the sounds these nights, I could trace spring's progress. A gentle night wind picked up, stirring the cottonwoods outside the window. If I studied the change in the voice of the wind in the branches from night to night, I would hear spring advance from the whoosh of bare branches to the whisper of baby leaves, to the full clatter of the leathery mature leaves.

I sat on, rejoicing in the rich unquiet of the country night, and it came to me that these sounds renewed me and gave me new life because they were the music of things charged with life – birds, animals, frogs and trees. It seemed to me that what our friend Jim heard in his city house were largely dead sounds of such things as traffic and the neighbours' radio and tv, lacking in the vitality I felt pulsing in the country.

I knew too, that what I heard would have continuing meaning for me. The ducks I heard earlier might have babies that I would watch with interest throughout the summer. The changing sound of the cottonwood leaves heralded shade I would value in summer. These cadences were a part of my life, not simply background music to lull me to forgetfulness. And oh, the beauty of them all!

Beekeeping beginnings

When I joined a beekeeping class last year my thoughts were all of summer and Yeats' bee-loud glade. A friend had kept a hive of bees at our place the year before, and, watching him calmly work the bees several times a month, I had become fascinated.

I saw new born bees pull their way out of their wax cells. I spent hours sitting on the sun-warmed rocks in front of the hive discovering how various were bee activities. I watched guard bees defend the hive entrance from wasps and spiders. I compared the different colours of pollen that the workers brought home on their legs.

The bees had been good to us, too. Fertilized by them, a very old plum tree beside the barn had, for the first time in seven years become loaded with fruit. When I worked in the garden that summer I was delighted by the life and fruitfulness the bees added, and that fall I had found that nothing could match the felicity of tasting fresh honey of one's own. In its amber were captured all the flowers of the past summer.

Sitting in a sterile, fluorescent-lit classroom, however, I became overwhelmed by the amount a beginner needs to know. While it's true that many hobbyists barely bother with their bees from one year to the next, content to take off honey only in good years, I felt close to the bees I would have, and already I was scheming for their good like an expectant parent.

Our March weekends became filled producing the surprising array of equipment required to establish two hives. First the boys and I fitted dovetails, nailed and painted ten wooden boxes or supers. Next the house became fragrant with the scent of beeswax when we set up a production line to nail and wire in the wax foundation for the hundred frames we needed for honey and broodraising.

Once our equipment was in order, I paced the land, looking for a site for the two hives. What I needed was shelter from the winter winds, early morning sun, good ventilation, closeness to water and a level site. I considered and rejected, imagining a flight path that would cut across our driveway (highly undesirable), picturing the sun's angle three months ahead. At last I called the boys to see the future home of Queen Mary and Queen Elizabeth (named by Morgan after Mary, Queen of Scots and Elizabeth I). When they had approved the little knoll I had chosen, protected from the northwest winds by a grove of wild cherry trees and close to a small pond, we wheelbarrowed our loads of freshly-made supers, hive stands, lids and wax-lined frames over and set them up.

A week later, the phone call came saying our bees had arrived and would we pick them up quickly, please. Full of elation, but not knowing what to expect, the boys and I hurried up to Fallbrook through a definitive spring day of fluffy clouds, brilliant fields, decorated with prancing lambs and calves. At last Queen Mary and Queen Elizabeth and their entourage were coming home.

The dusty, dim storage shed at the bee supply house was packed from ceiling to floor with bee cages; the air was filled with an extraordinarily vibrant humming of bees. I could scarcely hear the young assistant's parting instructions as he handed Morgan and Jeremy each a package. He coolly brushed off some of the attendant bees that were clinging to the outside of the screens and we sailed off into the spring afternoon.

Proudly the boys carried the boxes into the house. We had talked about bee voices and how they had different tones for different moods. In the car, their mood plainly had been hostile, but now we sprayed them gently with water, and the bees, thirsty after their long journey from the south, positively purred. We knew we should leave them in peace but their presence was hard to resist, and we all kept coming back to brood over them. Near nightfall, when there was less chance of drifting, we would hive our new arrivals.

Grasping the package of bees nervously, Morgan and I took up position beside the new hives. At that moment my six weeks of classes and preparations gave me no confidence at all. What I needed was experience and something told me that was not going to come easily. "One: open the package and remove the feed can. Two: pierce the candy plug in the little queen cage so the workers will release her. Three: suspend the queen cage between the frames," I rehearsed. Morgan gave me a weak smile and we were off.

The first time for anything is unpredictable. The feed can was tightly wedged and refused to slip up. We groaned. Morgan wiggled and pried at it nervously and we tried to remember that these were "tame" bees who really weren't as likely to sting as their angry humming suggested. At last the can shot out, and oh, how the bees spilled out in its wake. Desperately, I removed the separate queen cage and tilted the bees over the frames of hive number one. Thank goodness they settled into the hive willingly and did not take off.

Now for the queen. I planned to suspend her cage as instructed and let the worker bees chew out her candy plug to release her. ("Oh, Morgan, how ever will we get the nails to stay in this flimsy cage when we hang it?") Jeremy, who was lurking at a safe distance with a cowboy hat under his bee veil, was sent off home three times for nails, tacks, and finally, long straight pins. There. The cage finally was placed between the frames. We could close up that hive, and a good thing too, as it was really getting hard to see.

"Mom," Morgan said just as I placed the lid. "Weren't you going to put a pail of syrup in with them?" Blast. I removed the lid gingerly, adjusted things, and replaced the lid.

It was very nearly dark out by now. Jeremy was sent back for a flashlight, and Morgan and I sat down in the dusk. In the pond we could hear a pair of newly returned mallard ducks quacking above the resounding chorus of peepers. Already the buzzing in the hive was quieting to a hum.

Here was Jeremy holding the flashlight and we were ready for hive number two. This time the feed can emerged smoothly, and with some finesse, we tipped most of the bees over the frames. Wonderful! "It is essential to use as much speed as possible when completing these manoeuvres," I remembered the instructions from my class.

"Now for the queen, Morgan. I'll just puncture the plug…" Oh horrible, horrible and more horrible. The plug was gone. It must have been eaten on the long journey from the south. "Jeremy, for pity's sake hold the flashlight higher. Oh, how awful," I gasped. "She's out."

We watched the queen scuttle nimbly out of her cage and fly to the edge of the super. What would we do now? We had to have her. All our effort would be wasted if she escaped.

I gritted my teeth and pulled off my cumbersome protective gloves. As tenderly as I could, I grasped the queen by the wings and breathlessly slipped her well down into the hive bodys. Sweating hard in spite of the cool night air, I rapped the rest of the bees out of their package, Morgan added the feed pail, and together we placed the cover.

The three of us stood staring at our hives, aware of the night sounds again. A small flock of geese flew over our heads, hurrying to find a pond for the night. Instead of going home, we lingered, listening to the steadying hum of the hives. Questions nagged in the back of my mind – would the bees release the first queen in good time? Had I injured the second queen? In spite of it all, I couldn't help feeling triumphant.

Back at the house, Barry turned on the porch light and called to ask how we were doing and what was taking us so long. The boys headed home full of news, but I lingered on listening to the drone that sang of tree flowers and dandelions rich with pollen. Every spring would have a new savour for us now.

The rocks remain

Everyone needs a special place of retreat when things are hard, a place to be alone to think. When my family see me head out to my thinking place, the big stretches of pink granite that run through the fields in front of our house, they know I am not to be disturbed. I come to the rocks, the most solid and lasting thing I am likely to know, because I prize the sense of endurance that they give me. I come to the sunwarmed, rounded surfaces seeking their constancy and seeing in them the bones of the earth. For some time I sit drinking in the deep peace of the passive rocks, thankful to feel my mind turn from whatever external storms have sent me to this refuge.

"The rocks remain," I often mutter to myself, yet I never can help noticing that, written on their hardness is a history of violence and change. Running north-south are broad, dark scrapes of glaciers, marks that never fail to arrest me, no matter what problems I bring to sort out on the rocks. Seeing the scars that the grinding ice carved in the formidably hard rock, I can never be lulled into forgetting that our real foundation is change.

This violence of change that I read of in the granite has been brought home forcefully by recent volcanic eruptions. Within a span of years, as with the action of glaciers, or within days, as with volcanoes, the face of the earth in that area can change absolutely. In an odd way it pleases me to think that humans are not the masters of their surroundings that they would wish to be.

The flowing marks are all the more to be wondered at because they were caused by ice, ice which I usually do not associate with force, and it must have been a singular force indeed to imbed in such hardness traces that have lasted so many centuries. I stretch forward to stroke the glacial striations and imagine the strife these rocks must have faced.

The granite on which I sit so solidly has known fire as well as ice. An igneous rock, it began as a mixture of molten minerals within the earth. A billion years ago the liquid granite-to-be spewed up into air pockets that were made as the mountains of the Pre-cambrian Shield were formed. Once these low, rounded rocks lay within mountains that towered 4,000 meters. How the problems of a human shrink to scale before such a thought.

Signs of changes ahead lie before me at my feet as well. In the pockets of the rocks, grains of sand have collected. Even the hardness of exposed granite wears away. What were once mountains are now hills, and before my feet, as soil gathers and plant growth begins, are the signs of the new life that will form someday over the bare rocks.

Thinking of the rocks and the changes they have experienced, I cannot escape the thought that my own body is in harmony with the flux of the granite. How can I say I know my limits when I know also that all my cells will change completely and often during my life? How can I say that I am this or that? At any time within me is the possibility of change.

I sought the rocks for solace and answers, but, as always, I will leave them with the knowledge that my life is as secure as the variable wind that plays across my face or the very rocks at my feet. I don't know if I will ever be completely reconciled to this, but, participating in a small way in the life and death of mountains gives me much to be glad of.

Field evolution

The more closely I read the signs around me of the land's evolution the more it excites me. A tradition will be lost at my neighbour's farm now his cattle are sold, and I regret that, but now the land will be free to grow again, undominated by humans. The fields will take charge of their own future. By the process called "succession" they will sustain a series of communities of plants and animals until, more than a hundred years from now, where once hay blew in the wind, tall trees will reach.

When I look about me here at Foley Mountain I can read the first pages in the story of the path that the neighbouring fields will follow, for our fields, always unsuited to agriculture, have not been cut for more than a dozen years, and much has happened already.

Just as the first settlers cleared the land for farming, now pioneer plants such as milkweed and yarrow begin the changes that will make the fields a suitable place for the growth of trees. The wind takes their plentiful seeds and spreads them widely. These are seeds with endurance, and, if necessary, they can remain dormant in the soil for years until conditions are favourable. When they do find their time, though, they grow quickly.

In the secondary stage of succession, the one that I'm watching in our fields now, things move fast. Everything works to hold and build soil and to save moisture. Wildflowers bloom, matting the soil. Now longer-lived plants such as Queen Anne's lace and goldenrod appear. These two have the strength to withstand extremes of temperature, moisture and light. While they live they shade the soil, helping to keep it moist and when they die and rot they add to its fertility.

By improving conditions, however, the pioneers spell their own death. As they modify the environment, and they are able to do so quickly, they make a place for other plants, the woody-stemmed blackberries, juniper bushes and willows that will crowd and shade the pioneers. As the soil conditions improve, the first trees appear to fill in the field. Red cedar, white birch and poplar make their appearance.

With each change in the plant community the birds, animals and insects that live with it arrive. As the field and song sparrows move on to more open areas, the ruffed grouse appear.

During the first years we lived here, the growth of the trees was slow, but last year, for the first time I had the sense of walking through a woods. My view was cut short and I had to look upwards to the treetops just as I am learning to tilt my head to look at my teenaged sons. In fact, the young woods spreading through the fields here has much in common with teenaged awkwardness. The trees, untouched by long years of weather have not been shaped to character yet. They crowd the expanse of the fields in the same way my big sons crowd the limits of our small house. Still, I have only to look to the windswept trees at the woods' edge to rejoice again at being in on the birth of a forest.

Unfortunately, the saplings of these first trees cannot grow in their parents' shade, so soon the shade tolerant beeches, sugar maples, hemlocks and yellow birches that thrive in the fertile soil built up by previous communities will make their appearance. Unlike the time involved for the pioneers, each following stage will take longer, but the pattern is a steady one. Only a natural disaster such as the fire that ravaged "the Mountain" at the beginning of this century, or the intervention of man can interfere with this procession towards the richest and most diverse community of all, the mature woods. When, at last the tall trees have changed the fields to forest, conservation of soil and water will be at its best.

Looking out over the half-field, half-woods around me and rehearsing the stages it passes through, I feel a biblical quality to the simple rhythm of it all: "In the beginning there was...", "is now and ever shall be", "world without end." Yes, there is sadness when the hand of man leaves a field, but the regret should be tempered by thoughts of the flow of life that is undammed then.

First lessons with the canoe

Whenever I recall our disastrous first attempt at canoeing I am amazed that we have persevered. We were delighted when a friend lent us his great tin tub of a canoe. He said that if we could row a boat we would find that canoeing came easily. "Actually, you'll be surprised at how much easier you'll find canoeing," he said.

With visions of secluded northern waterways and loon calls, we bought a couple of books and studied strokes carefully. "J" stroke, "Jam Stroke" – it all looked reasonable and straightforward.

We didn't want anyone watching our first attempt, and, in our naiveté, we decided a large beaver pond would be a safer place for our venture than the nearby lake that was often wind-ruffled. Since we had told nobody of our plans, nobody had pointed out what we should have guessed: a beaver pond, with a murky bottom, the possibility of weeds, submerged stumps and unclear water was not a prudent starting place for beginners.

Only a few miles from home and conveniently bordering a lonely concession road, we found what we thought was a suitable place, and after heavy applications of mosquito lotion, we set off one May evening after supper. At first all went well. The wonderful sensation of eggshell lightness that you get the first time in a canoe after years in a stolid rowboat is unforgettable. We proceeded for the opposite shore in a series of erratic tacks, as we took turns compensating for our uneven rhythms. Once we got out of sight of the road, we could imagine that we were indeed moving into uncharted water. A family of teals swam away from our canoe, whistling and piping. Around a bend in the reedy shore a heron rose, startled and gawping indignantly at our awkward, splashing intrusion.

We advanced with growing confidence until we saw a figure come out of the bushes at the far end of the pond. "Oh dear," I said. "He's going to think we're awfully foolish." But it was worse than that. "Hey," the old man bellowed, "You froggin?"

We didn't understand. "Froggin?"

"Yeah. I know you're after them damn frogs in there. This here's my pond and I'll give you ten minutes to clear out or I'll be back with my shotgun," he yelled out drunkenly.

Catching bullfrogs was far from our minds, but now we had a real problem. We were quite willing to clear out, but could we? To do so we would have to turn, a manoeuvre we had not yet practised. Everything the texts had said about turning had fled from our minds. We were on our own.

Already the landowner was back, waving a whisky bottle in one hand and a shotgun in the other. Hurriedly we thrust our paddles in on the same side and dug in. We turned. Indeed we turned. Round and round we revolved while the man shouted and raged from the shore. Once, coming out of our spin temporarily, we even went backwards directly towards the infuriated pond owner.

I've often wondered since if he was suddenly confronted with the thought that his drunkenness had progressed further than he had realized. Plainly, if we were not crazy, he was.

We never did get the hang of a proper turn that night. Instead, through desperation, we developed a lengthening circle, which, much later, brought us to the roadside, shaken and sweaty. As we heaved the canoe onto the car top, we saw that our man had crouched over the rocks, cradling his shotgun and bottle and was moaning to himself.

It was not until we were well on the way home that I dared to tell Barry that I didn't believe the old man had any right to chase us away from the pond, which, after all, had direct access from the road.

As a turtle to water

At least once a year it happens that I rescue a turtle. Well, perhaps "rescue" is not the right word. Who am I to know to what goal a turtle aims? Who am I to reset its course, and, for that matter, can I guarantee its safety once I turn my back? I do know that painted turtles have been found to have a homing instinct that may well defeat me. When I pick up a turtle from the middle of a highway I am remembering our snapper. Perhaps, too, I am trying to balance scales which seem weighted against the rhythms of most of life at present.

We discovered the snapping turtle during our first spring here ten years ago and watched her for eight more years. At the end of May we would see her lumbering from the main beaver pond to the road, always taking the same resolute route to the sandy roadside. We were sure, with her size, she was old. The record for a snapper was seventeen inches long and fifty pounds. Ours was fourteen inches long and could have weighed thirty pounds, although, respectful of the turtle's reputation for finger severance, we never hefted her. Always, it was startling to see the ponderous reptile moving down the path.

Some years we were lucky and could bring a campground class to see the craggy turtle, often still pond-wet and draped with weeds. Sometimes we watched alone. With a profoundly broody presence, the snapper dug into the sand. Nothing deterred her, but there was nothing of haste about her digging either. She placed her clutch of eggs and covered them and withdrew. Over the day we came back as often as we could to watch her progress. When she left we always placed a stone near the turtle-raked sand and made a note on our calendar.

Unfortunately, the incubations rarely were successful. Often, before July was over, we'd find the nest ripped open, like many others we found around the Conservation Area. Fragments of leathery, whitish shell told the story. The raccoons had gained, but once again our hopes of more snappers for the pond were frustrated.

A couple of years ago, the turtle chose a particularly busy Saturday for her ritual. Every year we'd regretted her location, right by the most travelled section of the road. Now, when we checked on her at four, we found the magnificent turtle smashed by the roadside, her nest unfulfilled. I've hardly been able to believe she is gone, in the years since, so much was her presence a part of the seasons here.

I didn't know it, then, but I've read since that turtles have been reverenced by a surprisingly wide and differing group of cultures around the world. Both in Asia and North America, there are myths telling of turtles supporting the earth on their backs. Among the Iroquois and Hurons, the Great Turtle was master of the animals. The Mohawks went further and made their leading clan that of the turtle. Since the loss of our presiding snapper, I've come to understand a reliance on the solidity and deliberateness of turtles.

I think of turtles I have known, painted turtles, the dome-shelled wanderers, Blandings, and the peevish little mud-coloured musk or stink-pot. Pinned against my perception of each I see a smashed shell and jagged flesh and I know that, at the risk of being accused of harassment, I will continue to intervene. My rescues may not always have succeeded, but I hate to think that turtles, which have survived two hundred million years protected only by their shells, are now so vulnerable to humankind's speeded-up lifestyle.

When I take the current hissing, leaking reptile and escort it nearly to the water's edge, an interesting thing happens. The turtle catches (could it be a scent of?) water and there is no holding him. Unfailingly it heads for the water with such alacrity that I think the saying should be "as a turtle to water." It's an awareness of different kind of senses and instinct that makes the hoped-for preservation of turtles seem so worthwhile.

Summer

Sugaring for moths

Once I stood in an evening forest under a beech that shivered its leaves in the wind of an approaching summer storm and I waited. I had set up a lantern and I saw, as clearly as if already they were seized and pinned on my stretching board, the great moths I hoped to attract. I imagined the beige and wine-coloured cecropia, as big, then, as my hand, wings pulsing with life, lighting on the trunk of the beech. I saw her furred body and feathery antennae quiver as she waited, sending forth her scent widely in search of a mate.

Her need would be keen, I knew, as she would fly the night woods only for the span of a few brief evenings. Because she had no mouth parts, in her short adult life she would never eat. The cecropia had drawn herself from her cocoon only to reproduce. She would call males with the silent power of her scent, and for several hours she and her chosen mate would stay together on a log or trunk, deep in the richness of the forest. Then she would search for the trees that would best nourish her larvae, wild cherries, perhaps. Here she would lay her eggs and die. For a few nights the great velvety moth would glow in the woods, would seek and be sought, and then would fall as spent as the leaves at my feet.

A fretful wind caught at my hair and then dropped. I grasped my collecting net and waited, alive to the excitement of the sultry night. In a way, by seeking to have the moths within my grip I was reaching for passions I scarcely understood. To hold beauty and passion – the temptation was irresistible.

Again the wind gusted, tossing the whites of the leaves as if they were eyes rolling in fear. Distant lightning darted in the sky, brightening the leaves with whip-like flashes and I leaned forward, waiting for the "nightbirds" I was sure would come to my signal light. All my books had told me that they appear most readily before or just after a storm.

Perhaps the next time I glanced at the trunk it would be a luna moth I would see, the most exquisite of our big moths. She would quiver in waiting, bigger and better than my best specimen, the yellow tiger swallowtail butterfly that I had pinned in the centre of my case. Palest green, with lavender eyes, trailing her long tails behind her, she might at any moment now light before me.

And so I waited, with the air around me, at least in my imagination, peopled with moths. A few June bugs crashed into my lantern; a few smaller, indistinct moths flitted crazily around its light, but with movements too erratic for my clumsy sweep of the net. At last the storm intervened and I had to leave the woods without the moth I sought.

The next morning my father came to me holding out a large, beige form. "Is this what you wanted?" At last I had a cecropia, its wings stiffened and awkward in death, it was true, but I could relax them, arrange them. I turned and turned the handsome moth, searching it for signs of the dream moths I had imagined in the woods before the storm. Indeed, she was as beautiful as my books had promised. I softened and spread her wings and held her dead body in my hands, but it came to me then that all it was now was a lifeless form. None of my looking could make her into one of the wondrous moths of the forest. If I had robbed one of them of its short life, it too would be only a dead body on a pin. I placed her near the tiger swallowtail and looked at my collection with new eyes and found it wanting.

I never went out again with my net and my killing jar stayed empty from then on. To this day I never visit an insect collection in a museum without being reminded of the cecropia and the width of the span between life and death. I still take a lantern and some fermented mothbait on June nights, but now I go to celebrate life, not to end it.

Roadside spraying

It's that time of year again. One day you go out and the roadsides are dappled with flowers. The next day the flowers hang wilted, limp and dejected-looking, as if from a long-standing conflict with a severe drought. For more than a month afterwards the foul smell of herbicide will lurk along the ditches, explaining the diseased appearance of the once-lush foliage.

It may be true that roadsides no longer are troubled with patches of poison ivy and that fewer weed seeds harass the farmer, but we've paid a heavy price in terms of the diversity of wildlife and plants that used to flourish in relative harmony along the margins of the road. Roadsides weren't always this way, though. Come back with me for a moment to a road and its borders as I saw them one day thirty years ago.

The coming fall I would be going to school on my own for the first time, and, one high summer day, my mother decided the two of us would walk the route together so I would be familiar with it. We set off into the fresh morning with the lightness of two conspirators sneaking off together.

Our road passed through many little environments, and what stays with me is the astonishing abundance and variety of flowers and plants we passed along the way. First our road took us through deep woods. Out of the wet ditch grew plumy ferns, almost as tall as I was. Even although it was midsummer when birds sing less, I remember the birdsong from that sheltered ferny place. I sniffed the rich, woodsy scent happily as I scuffed through the gravel, following my mother.

After the first bend in the road, the woods opened out a little and we came to what my mother pointed out as the site of a pioneer home. She stopped to show me how to recognize the settlers' plants at the side of the road. There were glowing orange daylilies with ribbon leaves, sweet Williams heavy with the fragrance of cloves and a green and white striped grass.

At last we were out of the woods and walking past fields of buttercups, daisies and rolling cloud shadows. We never picked the scarce and fragile spring wildflowers, but the roadside flowers of summer were so generous that we could gather great handfuls to bring home, knowing they were sturdy enough to make the journey. I passed my mother a waxy buttercup and she picked some Queen Anne's lace, and laughing and delighting in the specialness of each flower, we moved on towards the school. By the time it came in sight we counted more than thirty different flowers in our bouquets.

My memory of that day ends with the two of us sitting down to rest on the warm ground and listening in perfect peace to the sound of the bees at work among the white clover and wild roses that grew in the sandy soil near the school.

At summer's end I walked that road to school and the map of its borders that I had formed that summer day was a comfort to me on my solitary walks. Each beautiful landmark – the ferns, the daylilies, the flower stalks, the rose bushes, now decorated with ripening rosehips – cheered me on my way each morning and welcomed me home each afternoon. The changing life of the roadside was the brightest part of my day.

Back now in the '80's, the spray truck moves relentlessly through the country, hissing forth its sickening poison. It dispenses death unthinkingly, in one place giving a farm protection against destructive weeds, in many others polluting and defiling the wild margins of abandoned farms and woods. It never fails to amaze me that in our brave new "high tech" world, the quality of life has deteriorated in so many ways and that people are willing to settle for so little in order to have their lives managed for them. The protest song "Where Have all the Flowers Gone?" is a song we may recall sooner than we realize.

Hanging clothes is fine

Hanging a line of washing isn't fashionable these days, whatever energy conservationists might wish. Almost anyone you asked would say they tossed things in the dryer, being much too busy for such a waste of time. Such is the prestige of being too busy for menial tasks that I hesitate to admit it, but I manage to cram a good deal of pleasure into my sessions with the clothesline.

I could say a lot about the art and craft of hanging clothes – the Zen of it, if you wish. As with all jobs, proper attention to detail does much to improve the quality of the procedure. For instance, running a clothesline keeps me finely attuned to the vagaries of weather. "Full many a glorious morning have I seen…" I mutter Shakespeare's sonnet under my breath as my fingers speed to peg the clothes, and I scan the red "sailors take warning" sky anxiously. Hanging clothes once is fine; dealing with rain-sodden ones a second time is quite otherwise.

Tension is important. After bitter experiences with snapped lines of wet clothes that draggled in the mud, I am as sensitive to the tightening of my clothesline as I would be to the tautness of violin strings.

In the same way, I give the wind consideration before I hang a line. On certain days of crazy, house-shaking wind here, a lineful of clothes in the morning leads only to clothes snagged in the plum tree across the yard by lunch.

The orderly progress of clothes along the line from weighty things first to light, quick-to-dry pillowcases last is a steadying business, but each labourer must know his limits, and I did think it was extreme when I caught a friend testing the wind with his finger, Boy Scout fashion, then securing his shirts, facing into the wind so that it filled them like sails. "They dry a little faster," he explained.

It's true that hanging a wash well is an art in itself, but what I find more important is the liberty that this routine job gives me. Although my feet are rooted to the porch floor, my thoughts are as free as the clothes-blowing wind. For instance, in the space of time required for fourteen pairs of socks and half a week's underwear to join the line I can toy with Gregory Bateson's theories of heuristics and ponder the latest bulletin from Amnesty International.

Just as my thoughts on the latter weigh me down, I catch sight of the three turkey vultures who ride our wind currents each day, canvassing the fields for carrion, and I am lost in the loveliness of their flight. At their present height, their scavenger heads and breath are not apparent, and I am reminded of the first time I saw a turkey vulture, flying in front of the sun so that it illuminated his wings and made me think of the primitive, symbolic birds of Indian paintings. Its silent, searching flight made it seem more to be feared than the red-tailed hawk with its harsh cries.

A gust of lilac-scented air blows around the corner of the house and sets the hanging wash to flapping. The line of clothes is progressing, as do my memories. Where once soft sleepers blew, now dangle long-legged blue jeans. Here is the shirt Jeremy coaxed out of me in an unguarded moment at the shopping centre, as loud and vulgar as the day he first coveted it. I had hoped that the sun would fade it to something at least a little easier to look at, but after many washings and airings, I've almost come to look at it as an old friend, one of Jeremy's treasures.

With the shirt up, my wash hanging is complete, and I must go back into the house, but this evening, just before the dew falls, I'll be back to gather everything in. The day will end with a resounding chorus of "Bringing in the Sheaves" as I carry my harvest of fragrant clothes, images and ideas indoors.

Heron census

Although the breeze was still cool, the rim of the sky was a heavy orange. Already we knew the day would be hot, but we also knew that there was no putting off our share in the heron census in which we had agreed to take part. This hot, muggy Wednesday of the last week in June was the last day we could visit the heronry and be sure of finding the birds at their nests.

In spite of the heat, Barry and I were looking forward to a day spent in the company of herons. We remembered the low-flying great blue heron who made his path over our house morning and night, and the glimpses we had of others lurking in the shallows of our beaver ponds, and we were glad of this day set aside to search for the primitive-looking birds in their colonies.

After wandering a lonely back road several times in a fruitless search for the landmarks listed on our sheet of directions, we stopped to consult a man sitting catching frogs from a flat-bottomed boat in a roadside swamp. While Barry was talking, I saw our first great blue of the day, as it cut its flight overhead and glided down among the elms farther into the swamp. The frogger said that he saw herons fly through that swamp quite often, but he doubted we could get at it without a boat. We withdrew and spread our topographical map over the hood of the car. If we followed a field that looked to be stretching in the right direction we could reach the back curve of the swamp by land.

Through the shimmering heat we trudged across the field, oblivious to the tapestry of field flowers, thinking only of the shade we would enjoy when at last we reached the scrubby woods. Unfortunately, we soon found out that the poison ivy, tearing raspberry canes, and dense mosquitoes within the woods made up for any coolness. The only thing that kept us scrambling up the rocky ridge the map had indicated as the last hurdle before the pond, was the great, squawking cries we began to hear.

At the tip of the ridge at last, we found we were at nest level, high over the swamp, and we realized we had a perfect view of a heronry of about twenty nests. Using binoculars, we watched the steady traffic of herons who appeared almost too large to negotiate the forest of drowned trees and too awkward to mount their basket nests. Sitting at treetop height, we could scan the babies in the nests waiting to be fed and watch their parents cruising in to feed them.

After the early summer greenery of the field, the swamp and its birds appeared mysterious and other-worldly. It was a place of dead trees weathered to ash grey, through which flapped the similarly silver-coloured herons. The only accompaniment to the strident heron talk was the gunking and screeching of an assortment of frogs in the sickly green skin covering the swamp, and the occasional knocking of a woodpecker on a hollow tree. In the menacing heat the sky echoed the colour of the trees and birds.

From our fine vantage point I began to dream of coming back to watch the herons on other days next year, mating, perhaps, and nestbuilding. But in reality I knew the birds must be left in peace if they were to survive, and that this must be our only visit. In the ironwood trees that hid us from the herons there was not a stirring of air. There was only the dead heat and a scene of birds which might have been seen near the dawn of the world.

The morning on the ridge was to be the highpoint of our census.

Although our other assigned colonies were not as difficult to locate, by afternoon we began to feel less hopeful about the herons' chances of survival in our area.

In a marshy field of buttercups we found one small colony of five nests, deserted except for an osprey that peered at us with what we thought was triumph. A third colony had been crowded out by a new housing development, and, the locals told us, the herons at a fourth large heronry had been destroyed in an afternoon by two unnamed youths with shotguns and a bottle of whisky.

What stayed with us as we drove home, though it was now only an image, was the memory of the morning's lofty birds in the steaming, primeval swamp. It was an image that now seemed to us to be threatened, and was one we didn't want to lose.

Through a child's eyes

School's out and now that my boys are free to wander outside every day it seems right to celebrate some of the outdoor things I would not have experienced fully without them. I count the chance to see things afresh with their eyes as one of the best gifts they have brought me.

In good times and bad, the children's fresh perception of the world has added depth to my life. The gift began when I watched a baby's eyes follow a bird's shadow across the room, and went on as I felt him bucking and waving in his back carrier in sympathy with the waving arms of a yellow birch tree.

I remember one black summer day when Jeremy was a baby and nothing, nothing worked to soothe his tears. In desperation I trailed out of the house with him and Morgan to look at the cottonwood tree on our lawn. At least I would appreciate a change of scene. There was a thunderstorm in the distance and the air was expectant. I stood taking in the coolness before the storm and then I realized that Jeremy, at long last, was quiet. While Morgan and I watched, he patted the deeply furrowed bark and muttered to the ants that swarmed over the ridges. Together we looked, and I hope will continue to do so for a long time to come. To see as a child sees opens you up to many perspectives. A tree observed upside down through your legs in the doubled-over posture of a three year old is an entirely different tree. Similarly, a field changes to a jungle if I look at it while lying face down beside a child.

While we peer through the dense spears of grass that reach high over our heads, we are almost certain to encounter a skulking bug of some kind. Never does an insect look more worth knowing than when it is presented to me on the outstretched, sticky palm of a three year old. Seeing how important the offering is to the child, I eye such a bug more thoroughly than I normally would, and, as a result, see what usually would escape my distant grown-up eyes, delicate lines of gold, or a metallic sheen, perhaps.

If my friend and I roll over, we can spend a very happy twenty minutes staring through a fringe of grass up to the distant sky. While we watch the clouds striding overhead and name their shapes, we may catch sight of a swallow and transform ourselves into birds, and, in our imagination, at least, become a part of the sky.

Upside down and ground level were the rule when the boys were little, but as they have grown they have stretched their horizons and so have I. With their encouragement I'm subduing my dislike of heights to go with them to treetops and barn lofts. No one really knows a pine who has not sat at its swaying summit listening to the wind. It's a pleasure for which I gladly pay with resinous hands that match the boys'.

I had to shorten my stride to match theirs, a feat that demanded all the patience I could muster. During my first snail's pace walks, I chafed and dragged, but eventually I learned to use the time to look around me more, to the point where now, on my brisk, solitary walks I catch myself wondering why everything looks less interesting. Walking quickly I may miss the pleasure of seeing a plump groundhog whisk into his hole, and I'm unlikely to notice that around our beloved old yellow birch a thicket of sapling birches is shooting up.

Now that they are older and I must work indoors often, I've got the boys trained to share their greater freedom with me. If Morgan finds a collection of walking stick bugs clinging to the back wall of the house, he calls me out to enjoy them; if Jeremy finds a catbird mother nesting in the plum bushes he lets me know. And in migration season, the call of "Geese, Mom, Geese!" comes to me so often that my work suffers but my spirits lift each time I dash out to see the passing flocks.

As I enjoy the pleasures of looking with children, I am reminded often of William Blake's lines:

To see a World in a grain of sand,
And a Heaven in a wild flower,
Hold Infinity in the palm of your hand,
And Eternity in an hour.

A passion for ferns

Lately I've been reading about the Victorians and their passion for ferns, a passion that does not surprise me. Once you start looking at ferns instead of passing them by in favour of the more obvious woodland features, you begin to realize just how much there is to excite you.

The Victorians became so enamoured of the grace and luxuriance that ferns gave their homes that the demand for imported tropical species as well as the less glamorous domestic types, became rapacious. As well as the live plants, decorative representations from pressed ferns to frond-garlanded wallpapers were everywhere. At the peak of the craze, one grower offered fifty varieties of the hart's tongue fern alone.

With the return of plants to homes and institutions, ferns are becoming popular again, but how many of us go out of doors to enjoy them in their natural habitats as well? Boughton Cob, in his *A Field Guide to the Ferns*, in the Peterson Series, points out that studying ferns is one of the easiest natural sciences to break into. The number of species in the area covered by the field guide is only about one hundred. Unlike birds, ferns stay in one place to be observed, and a leaf can even be brought home for closer study.

One of the interesting things about ferns is that they are everywhere – everywhere that does not have year-round ice, that is. There are ferns that are specially adapted to the Arctic's light and desert ferns that cling to the shade and moisture collected under rocks. Most wonderful of all, a fern-lover's dream, are the tropics where you can find not only the widest array of species, but also the curiosities: massive palm-like tree ferns, climbing vine ferns and the fragile and transparent filmy fern.

Most ferns do like damp and shade, and the local searcher will have the best luck in moist woodsy areas where, armed with only a good field guide and a hand lens, he or she can easily find a dozen of the most obvious types.

When you go looking for ferns, remember that they are much older than flowering plants. Fossils looking much like our ferns today evolved three hundred and fifty million years ago and rioted over the earth in the Age of Ferns two hundred and eighty million years ago. As non-flowering plants, ferns survive and spread by means of spores. These spores are as light as dust so their range of travel is much wider than that of seeds. They also have the ability to live for many years until conditions are right for them to engender reproduction. The birth of the ferns you see growing so lushly in many places is the result of a complicated two-step process that may take as little as two or three weeks or as long as fifteen or twenty years, although the average, curiously enough, is nine months, as it is for humans.

As you find new ferns you will be struck by the splendid diversity. What casual observer would imagine that the slight northern maidenhair with its fragile circlet of fronds supported on a black, hair-like stem and the bushy five foot cinnamon fern were in the same family? No matter how many kinds you find, the variations on the theme will still be fascinating.

After a few woodland excursions, you may be tempted to bring a few of your finds home. Ferns are not the easiest of wild plants to establish, but if you have a shaded, moist area and can provide good drainage and lots of leaf mould to satisfy their acid requirements, you have a good chance of enjoying ferns close to home. Take only a small portion of a clump, including a part of the underground rhizome, keep it damp and plant it quickly. Don't forget that you can bring ferns indoors too. Nothing is lovelier on a snowy day than a collection of choice, small, slow-growing ferns in a terrarium.

One very important caution: excellent as the Victorian appreciation of ferns was, it had a dark side. As parlours grew green, the countryside became denuded. Now, more than ever, as populations spread, the disappearance of some species is a threat. Don't be a fern robber. Never take a fern from the wild without the owner's permission. Always take only one and from a thriving stand.

Canoeing the Snake

When I had stumbled into my cold jeans at home that morning, our wish to paddle the river at sunrise had seemed like madness. Now, as I scrambled into my seat in the bow, still in a daze of sleep, I found myself remembering Kenneth Grahame's Water Rat in *The Wind in the Willows* describing his feeling for his river. He lived, he said, "by it and with it and on it and in it. It's brother and sister to me, and aunts and company and food and drink, and (naturally) washing. It's my world, and I don't want any other. What it hasn't got is not worth having, and what it doesn't know is not worth knowing." By travelling the river stealthily with a canoe in the earliest morning Barry, our friend Clayton, and I hoped to come closer to the river as the Water Rat might have seen it.

Clayton pushed off and we began our path downriver. The Snake (we laughing called it "the mighty Snake" was true to its name, an alluring river that, in its curves and bends, made the longest distance between two points. Only in spring was it passable by canoe. In summer it became merely a damp path between long pools. I doubt if anyone else ever saw any reason to travel its length, but for us it was like a thread of rich life looping in secret through the fields.

At first we paddled through river mists, watery sounds and shadow trees dreaming in the dim light. In order to find yourself, or, in this case, the river, you must lose yourself, I mused. In the light, blowing mist that formed and reformed the scenes we passed, time lost its sense.

When we found a current, Barry and Clayton put down their paddles and we drifted, at the will of the stream. Not one manmade sound broke in on us in our swaying path towards the lake and light.

We moved in our dream from bend to bend, here to a bay dappled with lily pads, there past islands dense with unfurling fern fronds and all the while the strengthening light made the river mirrors clearer. In the calm water stretches, reflected trees grasped at us. A muskrat, a water rat, cut in front of the canoe swimming purposefully towards the water lilies. Briefly the channel of his wake remained and then it was erased as the first wind of the morning sent tiny shivers across the river. The wind was up and now splinters of warmer light came through the trees above the line of the mist.

The canoe followed a bend and we came out on the broadest stretch of water so far. Suddenly, ahead of us a solitary great blue heron rose unwillingly out of the tree uttering his primitive croaking call. From bend to bend he flew ahead of us, with measured beats like a mystical bird drawing us farther and farther down the river.

Now the quiet stream passed through a field where a burst of light from the newly risen sun warmed us. On the opposite bank a small herd of cattle had waded through the shallows and stood up to their knees in river and morning light like a scene from an old Dutch painting.

The canoe passed into the trees again. Although the woods was close-set, we knew we were nearly at the river's end. It began to gather itself and pick up speed as if it, too, knew it was close to the lake. And then, on a ripple of current we drove the canoe forward and out into the lake where the new sun hitting the water made it dance with curls of mist. High above our canoe the heron flew with steady wings.

Ahead of us remained a stiffish paddle back up the Snake, but we did not care. The words of the Water Rat were our words, "…there is nothing – absolutely nothing half so much worth doing as simply messing about in boats."

The Thunder Bird

The first time I saw him I thought I had found the Indian Thunder Bird. A shadow scudded across the sun and I looked up to see a black-winged bird sail by on wings large enough for an eagle. I stopped my car and jumped out. This was a magical bird. I watched how his black-brown wings caught the light. Now he tilted and dipped on wings held at the V, now he soared letting the wind take him. Never had I seen such gliding! For more than half an hour I stared until the bird drifted out of sight.

In the many years before I saw another, I thought of the bird as a special hawk. I was still at a stage where hawk identification was a hopeless muddle and I knew better than to search for a name of a bird that had appeared to me only as large and brown. In my excitement over his graceful flight I had not even tried to look for field marks.

But when I came here I found out that my Thunder Bird, although a bird of prey, had not been a hawk. I was disgusted to find that the prey he had sought on those magnificent wings, was, in fact, carrion. My primitive hunting bird was a mere turkey vulture. When I confessed my discovery to Barry, he laughed, remarked on the scavenger's ugly, featherless, red head and asked if I had ever smelled the foul breath of a low-cruising vulture.

Three turkey vultures visit Foley Mountain most years, although their roost is a few miles farther north. After my first disillusionment, I kept coming back to the great beauty of their flight and I took the time to find out more about these unpopular birds.

In the first place, I learned that it is thought that all raptors, or birds of prey evolved from the scavengers. Of these, kites are the most primitive, but turkey vultures are birds of antiquity as well. Furthermore, they have the largest distribution of the raptors, being found from extreme South America to southern Canada. I found that I had been right to compare my bird's flight to that of an eagle, as their wing span is nearly the same. Although the vulture weighs only four and a half pounds, this relative of the condor has a wingspread of seventy inches, about as far as my outstretched arms can reach.

Always cursed by the give-away carrion odour he carries with him, the turkey vulture is particularly secretive in his choice of nest areas. The eggs are usually laid in limestone fissures and caves or in hollow logs and stumps, and both parents incubate them for about a month. Two young are born, and, unlike those of most other predators, they are alert and able to see right from their first day. Because they too feed on carrion, in their case regurgitated for them by their parents, the latter have to be particularly wary of predators likely to be attracted by the strong stench.

It is to their wonderful flight that I return, though. Dependent as these birds are on the quality of air currents to keep them aloft and travelling, the sacrifice of remaining close to earth for that month of child-rearing must be considerable. According to Roger Tory Peterson, the humble turkey vulture is the greatest of all the gliders. Sun-warmed rising air can lift a vulture swiftly one thousand feet into the air without a wing-beat.

And so, after my squeamishness at the thought of their diet, I have been forced to admit that vultures are as worthy of respect as any other birds of prey. They are cleansers and healers, keeping the land safe by cleaning up carcasses that might otherwise breed and spread disease. For me, the turkey vulture is still chief of the birds. In his tilting flight he may be seeking the odour of something I would find repulsive, but such is his command of the air in doing so that I can imagine thunder in his wings and lightning flashing from his hooked beak. I never feel closer to being airborne myself than when I watch him.

Again and again

Again. And again. And again. Three times in quick succession we heard the car spin its tires in the gravel and reverse on the dusty road up near the campground, one hot Sunday afternoon. Barry looked up at me from his tea, slapped the cup down and took off for the truck without a word. As he left off I could hear the car spin once more and take off for the park gates, and I bit my lip. Since the park is out of the mainstream of traffic and away from cities, trouble is mercifully rare, but each act of vandalism is still infuriating and needless.

Barry returned soon carrying the long and battered body of a black rat snake, a threatened species in Ontario. Seeing the snake sunning itself on the road, the driver must have deliberately run it over, not just once but repeatedly with a malice we found hard to imagine. A crazy squeal of brakes and a beautiful snake had been obliterated. For the rare, five foot long snake, with his dark, dappled skin was beautiful. I reached out and stroked the still warm body and then turned away.

The fear of snakes: we are confronted by it often in the park and no amount of information seems to reassure those who have it. Countless times we have repeated: there are no poisonous snakes in eastern Ontario. We live in one of the fortunate areas where snakes are harmless. You can feel free to walk anywhere in safety. But still we find snakes dead, run over intentionally, hit by a rock, or even beaten with sticks, and all in the name of fear.

"Do you blame me?" a kindly old man who would never hurt anything else asked me once, "When I was a kid my older brothers picked up some snakes and tied them around my neck and shut me in a cellarway. When my mother found me it took her two hours to settle me down. To this day, if I see a snake I have to kill it. I just can't stand seeing them around."

Most people who fear snakes can't explain their fear with a story like that, but the fear is no less real for them, so real, in fact, that I am taking a chance simply by writing this piece. Some years ago I wrote in the local paper about the park's good fortune in having some of these rare snakes, only to be told time and time again that many people now would never visit Foley Mountain for fear of running into those awful big snakes. Let me hasten to add that your chances of meeting one are slight. Last year, for all I am out very often, and always watch for black rat snakes, I never saw one. As with any snake you might meet in this area, a quick aggressive gesture is all you need to send them on their way. Unfortunately, they have every reason to fear humans.

The good news is that we've learned that the fear of snakes can be overcome with understanding. If Barry happens to find a snake on a teaching day he brings it along to show the visiting class. Of course, no one who is fearful is forced to come near, and at first there may be a few "ugh's" and screams, but, as the facts come out, and they see Barry handling the snake with enthusiasm, the great majority of children do become interested. "Who could dislike a snake who does the farmers so much good by being more effective as a rat killer than cats?" he will ask. Then he tells them how a snake is so helpless it cannot move unless the temperature is warm and shows them how the snake can bluff by rattling the tip of his tail under a leaf in imitation of a rattlesnake, although he has no venom to back up his defence. After a few more anecdotes he asks if anyone would like to touch the snake gently before he lets it go. It is a rare child who refuses.

The snakes with which Barry has delighted school children are warm with life, but not so the black rat that he tossed sadly into the field that Sunday. Soon there may be none of these harmless giants left to exert their valuable control on vermin. As always, out of fear comes destruction.

A rabbit in the house

When first confronted with a rabbit to go with our three cats, dog and skunk, I built her a cage, a fine, roomy cage for a young rabbit, I thought at the time. It didn't work. I don't like to say Bun declined to use it. In the first place she grew. In fact, she rapidly grew to be far larger than I had imagined a rabbit could be. And as she ventured out to make our house her own, I had the impression that she had decided that she was not made for cages.

Bun, the prize my son Morgan won in a kindergarten Easter lottery, is not the usual fluffy little white and pink bunny; she is a veritable grey dragon of a rabbit. As far as looks go, I'm sorry to say an unkind friend has likened her to a cow pie. And indeed, there is no denying that she has a stout and spreading figure. But then any rabbit who begs standing up on her hind legs as shamelessly and persistently as she does is bound to be heavy. Actually, I find her appearance beautiful. She is silver grey, distinguished with darker markings on her face like watered silk. Her silky ears are charcoal-rimmed as well. I also find Bun's voicelessness admirable. In a house of Siamese cats, a rabbit is surprisingly silent. She does delight the boys with a resonant growl if teased, but, other than that, her vocabulary consists of a whirring noise that denotes affection.

In the beginning the idea of a rabbit free in a house did not seem unreasonable. We fenced her in the kitchen with a leftover child-proof gate and placed newspapers in a corner of the kitchen for her. Sharing the kitchen with a rabbit, I learned is not altogether a bad thing. Bun is a creature of whims. One minute she'll be spread out in a sun patch asleep. The next she'll take a notion and make an ungainly dash for the water pail. If she feels loving she will charge across the room and bury her head in my feet, whirring mightily. There is nothing more steadying in time of trouble, I discovered, than a solidly loving rabbit.

Nevertheless, when Barry strongly suggested that it would not hurt Bun to spend her summer out of doors, I was ready to agree. If she had been willing to accept the kitchen as an extended cage she would have been welcome to stay. Unfortunately, she observed the cats and her friend, the dog, coming and going freely, and decided to take over the house. When Barry carried the stoutly kicking Bun out to her new summer quarters I knew I wouldn't miss her rowdy forays on the house.

For a few months telephone and vacuum cords would remain untested by rabbit teeth. I would not need to respond to the ominous gnawing sounds that meant Bun had once more escaped and was re-shaping the furniture. I was still nursing the indignation I had felt when she first mastered our stairs, giving her access to the entire second floor. Greatly pleased by her new feat, she had spent a lot of time bounding upstairs and the boys had spent a similar amount laughing, reproaching her, carrying her back down and cleaning and repairing. And then, on a day when I was home alone, I heard Bun upstairs and groaned. Only a minute ago she had reposed near my feet; the gate was securely in place. How could 'the varmint', as the boys had taken to calling her, have squeezed out again? My breadmaking was at the critical stage and I simply couldn't leave it to retrieve the wily wretch. With mounting dismay I worked away over the dough, listening to the sounds of scurrying and galumphing, wondering where the piles of rabbit raisins would be this time, and what electrical repair work would be necessary. Really, this was worse than having little kids home again. Then I heard it: first a flopping noise, and then an unmistakeable bumpety-bumpety noise. Trailing flour, I made a dash for the stairs and there was Bun sitting bemused at their bottom. It seemed she had learned a lasting lesson that rabbits may ascend stairs capably, but do poorly in the return descent.

Unfortunately, the end of her visits upstairs only gave her more time to devote to the main floor. Rabbits appear to me to live in a circular fashion. Their reasoning is in circles – always returning to the original point, as in, for example, the acquisition of food. Their favourite path is also circular. In my frequent attempts to persuade her to return to the kitchen I found she would play 'ring around the rosy' with me in the rest of the house for exactly as long as I was prepared to keep it up. Often I wielded a broom, the better to steer her, but rabbits are warlike creatures, and Bun reshaped many a broom for me, growling and tossing her head as she boldly snatched out handfuls of broom straws.

What prompted Barry to recommend a summer outside, though, was frustration over garbage. This manoeuvre was the only time rabbit and skunk teamed up. Fanny has, as the school psychologists might say, "problems with aggression" which leads to a distressing tendency to sneak up on Bun when she's resting (rabbits do a lot of resting) and snap at her tail for the sheer pleasure of it. When it came to opening a door and pulling over the kitchen garbage, however, the skunk found it well worth her while to forget her vendetta. Bun's superior weight for tipping the garbage can meant that hardly a night went by without a skirmish that lead to well-picked over garbage littering the kitchen floor. Actually, with their disparate tastes they made an excellent, Jack Sprat-ish team. What one disliked the other relished.

Quickly Barry and I built a spacious, airy cage on stilts, facing the morning sun, sheltered by a thicket of old plum bushes near the house. Any time I had qualms about the exile, I reminded myself that rabbits are supposed to live outdoors. If it hadn't been too cold for her and too solitary in the unheated barn in winter, she could have lived there year-round. The new summer cage would be cooler for her in summer, and, presumably, healthier. Anyhow, the house was looking tired, and I was tired of outwitting rabbits.

Once out, Bun seemed smaller, yet we found her presence still was commanding. It turned out that we all gravitated to the hutch in summer with offerings. For with the coming of Bun we had learned a new appreciation of all vegetation as potential food, from the first clover in May to the last dandelion in December. From her summer vantage point the rabbit graciously accepted offerings from plum leaves to carrot tops.

Undaunted by her new situation Bun held court with our own animals and the local wildlife. It may have been our imagination that made us think more birds visited the plum thicket that summer. But there was no mistaking the attentions of a bullfrog who spent several hours a day mooning below the hutch. Tana, the old black hunting cat, brought her kills and laid them out in front of the cage for Bun to inspect. Whether this was to show them off or to crow about Bun's temporary caged state I cannot say. As for Grog, he was in faithful attendance. When we had first introduced the rabbit to the kitchen we had had doubts about how he would treat her, considering how regrettably fond the dog is of chasing wild rabbits out of doors. We had pointed out to him firmly, though, that this particular rabbit which was now sharing his favourite lair under our kitchen table was not to be harassed, and he had accepted it. In fact, he seemed to look on her as a pet. They slept together under the table at night; he growled if we rebuked her loudly for her chewing habits, and, if the skunk attacks proved too distressing, she ran to him for protection. Now he made the hutch his first and last stop of the day, exchanging whiskered conversation, and often rested nearby.

The hottest days Bun lay like a beached whale, receiving her visits languorously, but when the weather was temperate the boys let her out for a walk. The first of these, back when dandelions bloomed in our dooryard, had been sedate. The rabbit reminded me of "mostly in clover" as she dazedly ate her way through her walk, scarcely knowing which bloom to attend to first. Later, confidence and the end of dandelion season brought out the worst in her. Walks became wild dashes (rabbits are given to whims and sudden starts and explosions) with the boys – dashes that lead to one of two kinds of disaster. Either she darted into the depths of the plum bushes, giving Jeremy (the only one small enough) the prickly misery of hauling her out or she scurried directly for the forbidden wealth of the vegetable garden. One day Bun found she had a new fetching pink harness and leash and that her walks, perforce were of a more restricted nature.

These recent days of heat make heavy going for Bun even in her shady palace in the plum bush thicket, but heat, we've learned, is the only condition rabbits do not face bravely. Soon, however, it will be summer's end and Bun will return to the house again. Surprisingly, so powerful is her personality that I find myself looking forward to the event. For a few weeks before she fully realizes how much she can get away with, she will be a meek rabbit. Then, on the first chilly night, her whiskered face will peer around the kitchen door; she will ruminate. In the living room I will be reading aloud to the boys, with Grog basking on the rug at our feet. The scene is too alluring even for a chastened rabbit. Within minutes she will tiptoe into the living room, tilting her scut of a tail as if to say "I have as much right here as any dog." She'll allow herself one gleeful circle of the rug and then settle beside Grog, imitating his outstretched forepaws. Soon we'll be joined by the cats – all spread around the rug. And before the read is over, there will be a thunk as a half-dormant skunk drags herself heavily from her house, and a patter as she, too, gravitates to the living room and the rug. "The peaceable kingdom," I think to myself in wonder as I glance from the book.

Northern orioles

When the northern orioles took to nesting in the cottonwood tree outside our house we were delighted. As elms, beloved by these birds for nesting trees, fell prey to Dutch elm disease, many experts predicted a decrease in the beautiful orange and black birds. The shapely elm at the end of our lane where we had seen a pair of orioles nest for four or five years, sickened and shed its branches until it looked like a gallows tree. Gaunt and dead, it held on for another year and another brood was raised, then, in a scant wind on a January afternoon it clattered to the road, leaving a gap in our horizon. Limp on the snow lay the silky grey pouch of the oriole's nest, and that, we believed was the end of that.

For a year we missed the brilliant birds moving like a vivid thread through our summer's greenness. Then, one breathlessly steamy day last May, I saw a flash of orange among the cottonwood leaves. Over the next few days there were other reports of the oriole being seen near the house. "I heard his song when I was raking under the tree, Mom," Morgan said. "You know that bright, warble, cheery like a robin's, only higher?"

"That orange bird was back on the wire in front of the house," said Jeremy. "It looks like he's staying here."

By the end of a week it was confirmed. Standing under the cottonwood looking up, Barry saw a hanging nest. For a few weeks we would have to avoid the spot for fear of disturbing the nesting female, and we would worry until the nestlings were safely fledged. To have nesting orioles so close to the house, though, was a joy that made a temporary absence from our trees worthwhile.

Each morning I woke to hear the gay song outside my window. Each evening I sat safely out of the way watching the birds dashing into the tree like fiery streaks. Jeremy had saved the old nest from the fallen elm and sometimes I fingered it thoughtfully, admiring its pliant strength and picturing the new nest in our tree.

In a couple of weeks we heard sounds of babies and the tempo of darting in the cottonwoods increased. We were looking forward to the first flight of the young shortly. But then came a night and day of heavy rains and the unexpected happened. At tea time the following afternoon Jeremy came rushing in to tell me that the nest with its babies was lying at the foot of the tree. Our orioles had come back to us, but now it looked as if they would fail in their new nesting tree.

I looked out at the nest and thought hard. Somehow I must try to mend the damage to it and rehang it in the tree. Morgan went to fetch a stepladder, and I hunted out some fine but strong linen thread that I hoped would imitate the grassy support work of the nest. As a weaver I had always admired oriole nests. Now I would try my hand at blending my weaving with the birds'.

I took up the nest of warm, wriggling babies and began my darning, seriously hampered by the attacks of the parent birds. I was glad to see that the babies were mature and well-feathered and thus nearly ready to fend for themselves. My work would only have to last a few days before they would take flight.

My weaving complete, with the boys steadying the ladder and my thread clutched in my teeth, I carried the nest up to the bough amidst the hissing protests of the babies and the violently hostile attacks of the parents. A few lashes with the thread, a tug on the nest to test its strength, and I had the infants restored to their hanging home in the tree. Then I retreated thankfully down the ladder with my face shielded from the parents' fury.

Would the repaired nest be accepted? Within an hour the parents' distress had subsided. They had resumed regular visits to the nest with beaks full of caterpillars, visits that continued for just two more days. Then the young found their wings.

Now the flamelike grace that had filled our tree was gone. Oriole song no longer began my mornings. The new lives that had literally hung by a thread all were dispatched safely. But the nest remained, I am proud to say, through the worst of the winter winds that followed, and I look on it as a promise that where one nest could hang another may be built.

A field of tall grass

Happy the woman who looks out on a field of tall grass at full blow. Such a field begins after a heavy rain on a steamy, hot day in May, with grass spears thrusting up two inches in a single day. In haste it grows on until, by June's end, the grasses ripen and reach wading depth. To the tune of the slightest breeze they swish and sing.

At dawn, wakened early by birdsong, the woman stands on her porch watching wisps of mist fade from the field before the rising sun. A swallow, its wings warmed by the sun, skims the field seeking insects. "Lyrical, lyrical, lyrical," calls a sparrow from the heart of the grass. Hanging from the grass, dew-limned spider webs shimmer in the day's first wind. The woman turns back into the cool dimness of the house.

After breakfast, from her doorstep, the woman watches the two boys and their dog rolling and swimming in the field's grassy waves. The three snap and snarl at each other like puppies in early summer delight, flinging themselves headlong into the billowing grass. In the stiffening wind the grass shakes its tassels of pollen over the three, touching their play with golden dust.

By the time the woman reappears at the back door with washbaskets, the sun has moved higher in the sky and the boys, having encountered a hidden patch of thistles, have given up their rolling for the gathering of thatch. She sees two walking sheaves of grass stagger through the field to the bare rock further down the field. Encouraged by the dog, they assemble the sheaves into a large mound, remotely suggestive of a grass hut.

"Killdeer, killdeer," the crooked-winged killdeer skims the field, giving forth the lonesome freedom of his call at noon when the woman stands at the edge of the rushing grass to call the boys for lunch. How confidently the field birds navigate the sea of grass, the woman thinks to herself while she listens for the sounds of her boys. But now all the birds of the field fall quiet and the woman can hear only the song of the grass. A marsh hawk, wings poised over his grey back at a "V", is hunting the swampy grass of the lower field, silently gliding close to the ground in his search for prey. She watches the hawk cruise in to land in an apple sapling. Here he hovers searching the now-silent field of grass, only to be driven off when the boys struggle noisily homewards across the whole breadth of the field. In their wake tunnels the panting dog, making huge bounds now and then to get his bearings in the deep grass.

In the late afternoon the woman brings a bowl of beans out to slice on the bench overlooking the field and follows with her eyes the paths the wind makes through the dancing grasses. Three beans evenly sliced, one glance outwards across the field to the sky's edge and back, she allows herself. The grass shadows on the laneway are lengthening now.

When at last the evening light slants across the stilling grass, the woman makes one final, lingering trip to the field. This time she walks idly along the path that leads through the field to the orchard, heedless of the harshness of the grass that cuts at her bare legs. She is followed by her lean, black cat who bounds from stone pile to stone pile, now dabbling at hunting, now rushing a grasshopper, and, like the dog before her, leaping high to get a view over the grass. The woman sees, but does not point out to her cat, the dried ball of grasses of a mouse nest close to her feet, and moves on, admiring the rich variety of life the field of grass nurtures. As the woman walks over the field at evening, each blade catches the sun, leading her onward, seemingly forever, through the burnished, grassy sea.

Barn swallows

Barn swallows, among the last migrants to arrive here, and the first to gather into a flock and leave, are pure essence of summer. Their time with us may amount to only a scant twelve or thirteen weeks, but while they invade the air around our small farmhouse they are very much in evidence.

Because our house is exposed and offers few nesting sites, we find ourselves wondering each year if we will face a swallowless summer, yet every year three or four pairs return to fill the air with their dashing and chattering. Will they accept their old, daubed-mud nests in the porch rafters this time, or will we have to walk over to the barn to see swallow babies, with their short tails and silly, gasping mouths? But after a few days of swallow faces studying us earnestly through our kitchen window, a few days of vocal consultation over the mud-spattered porch ledge, they accept last year's nest and begin work on its improvement, or they arrange a fresh start beside last year's cup.

When they were little, my boys had a horrid, exuberant song: "I like mud, grunt, grunt," they chanted as they returned from the mudpuddles at the end of a fruitful day. I am reminded of it now that mud is at a premium and we and the swallows rejoice in rain with its subsequent mud puddles. A choice patch of mud, as the swallows and the boys recognize, is a fine thing.

At this point we all become aware of the burden that resident swallows can be. The three cats, always ardent birdwatchers, will now be confined to the house until the babies are fledged. They spend much time at the window, staring at the nestbuilders so heavily that they sometimes forget the intervening glass, and, in a burst of excessive enthusiasm, smack their heads against the window.

Nest-building seems to require an extraordinary amount of swallow conversation. Glad as we are to have these birds so intimately with us, their unceasing chatter becomes unnerving. We have stopped using the kitchen door leading to the porch and are resigned to longer trips around the house, but when a swallow drives me from the clothesline I am indignant. Later in the day a series of bird droppings is added to the message that it is now we who are the territorial invaders.

It is a difficult lesson. Every year Grog, our border collie, has to learn again that swallows are not within the scope of herd dogs. There comes a day when nesting begins in earnest and, with much broodiness, the swallows settle to guarding their eggs. Grog, who resents being forbidden the porch with its superior view of kitchen activity, never learns from past experience. Each year he tries again to round up the swallows as they leave the nest so he can herd them off far past the barn. The swallows, remaining for their part hopeful that they will drive the fool away from the precious eggs permanently, are quite willing to be chased at a lunatic gallop round and round the yard, since it keeps him away from the nest.

Considering the hazards they face, our swallows have done well with their nests, generally adding three teetering children to the midsummer lineup on the telephone wire. Sometimes they even manage a supplementary batch who take flight only days before the little flock flies south in mid-August. Only occasionally do we come upon a crumpled little death on the porch floor, and once the biology student, Sinbee, who was looking after our house for us, was able to salvage a nestling fallen from a collapsed nest. When he found a well-developed, still-living baby on the ground, he made a home for it out of a berry-box lined with a Kleenex, and suspended it from the clothesline. There, he told us, the parents fed it and encouraged it for several days until it took flight.

With the worries of surrogate parenting gone, the few weeks of free flight that follow are filled with pleasure as we watch the mature swallows take freely to the air, no longer hampered by family concerns. Nothing is closer to the heart of summer than swallows skimming over a cloud-dappled hayfield.

The stone garden

For years I've wrestled to coax the flowers of my choice to grow here. I've watched my peonies, with roots in skimpy, sandy soil, produce only three or four small flowers in spite of my loving care and efforts to improve the soil. Foxgloves, lilies – I've tried all my favourites and often have been disappointed as they dwindled and died. At last, though, I'm learning to take close note of what flowers are happy here and to enjoy their appropriateness. Now I look forward to the lemon-coloured day lilies, the satiny hollyhocks and the luminous bed of poppies that flourish unasked each year. Sometimes I weaken and plant a rosebush, trying to be content with its few slight flowers, but mostly I have learned to go with the prevailing conditions. In some cases this has brought about a whole new appreciation of common flowers I previously ignored.

There is a logical extension to all this, of course. Some days I ask myself why I trouble to grow flowers at all when the fields and woods are so generous with wild ones. Are the cornflowers that nod in my garden more to be enjoyed than the celestial blue of the unfortunately-named viper's bugloss? Perhaps some day I'll be able to content myself with the uncultivated garden that is all around me.

When I think about my surroundings of field and woodland

gardens, I often think of the stone garden. There is a south-facing granite ridge far back in the park that I like to visit. Its attraction is, I suppose, an acquired taste. Friends have stood with me at its summit and told me they found the sloping rocks bare and uninviting. The first time I came out of the woods I too did not appreciate the place for itself. In the beginning I came back for the splendid views I got standing on the ridge, or, like the many animals and birds whose traces I detected, I came on my way to somewhere else. It was not until a hot July afternoon when I was picking blueberries out of the patches that nestled in the rocks that I began to think of the bare stones of the ridge as a garden.

If I had not been reading a book on Japanese landscape gardens at the time, perhaps I would never have discovered the loveliness of the place. It began when I paused in my picking and looked out at the stunted oak trees that clung to the ridge. In the past I always had averted my eyes at the sight of these trees. They were so unlike the sturdy giants that grew in the woods that, if it had not been for the characteristic bark and leaves, I would not have recognized them for what they were. It was a wonder that they survived at all, given the lack of soil and water, plus the lack of protection from sun, wind and cold.

The unfortunate trees even called down lightning, standing as they did, isolated on the bare rocks. This time, however, I saw these trees as beautiful in their deformity, much in the same way as Japanese bonsai trees are beautiful, although the oaks had been shaped to their interesting gnarls by nature rather than man. Then I began to apply what I had seen to the rest of the ridge. The rounded granite rocks in themselves were lovely. Their flecks of quartz caught the sun and their rosy colour blended handsomely with the blue and bottle greens of the lichens and mosses. In the best Japanese tradition, this ridge was a garden of simplicity. Once my eyes had adjusted to its scale, I realized that the large, sparely-filled frames of the rocks made each small beauty, each diminutive flower or grass stand out.

I turned my attention back to the blueberry patch, the fruit of the stone garden, and let my eyes travel slowly over the patterns of the leaves and the colours of the berries at different stages of ripeness. The stone garden had evolved over many lifetimes to its present dappled loveliness and I knew it had a quality my gardening skill could not have matched.

Henri Fabre

When I was at the height of my enthusiasm for collecting moths and butterflies, I happened on Henri Fabre's chapter on the peacock moth and I took to the man instantly. Here was a man who understood. Here was someone who, from the sound of his account was an ordinary person, not a lab-coated scientist. Yet this man looked at the smallest details of his world with a passion that exceeded my own. Not only that, but he appeared to have a masterly plan for studying his beloved insects, a plan that gave him excellent results. Best of all, he wrote good stories:

> We enter the room, candle in hand. What we see is unforgettable. With a soft flick-flack the great Moths fly around the bell-jar, alight, set off again, come back, fly up to the ceiling and down. They rush at the candle, putting it out with a stroke of their wings; they descend on our shoulders, clinging to our clothes, grazing our faces. The scene suggests a wizard's cave, with its whirl of Bats. Little Paul holds my hand tighter than usual to keep up his courage.

I remembered the drama of his descriptions all the years I was growing up.

When, as an adult, I went to the library in search of his works, I was surprised. As a pioneer insect-researcher and a notable story teller, I expected to find at least a few of his books. Instead, the card index showed that there was no Fabre at all. Finally, I tracked down some of his work in secondhand book stores and settled down to see how his writing would appear to a sceptical grown-up.

I had not realized the exigencies under which the Frenchman had lived. I learned that there was a darker side to the life of the man who appeared so energetic and enthusiastic in his writing about insects. For forty years Fabre had "fought with steadfast courage against the paltry plagues of life" before he could find time and peace to pursue his insect studies. Because he received only a pittance for teaching primary school and had a large family to support, it was not until he was fifty-five that he could afford to buy a house and two and a half acres of sun-baked, thistle-clogged land for his "laboratory of living entomology". In his poverty, his only equipment was a hand lens; his best instruments were, he said, time and patience.

He was eighty-four when he published the last of his ten volume, 2,500 page record of the history of insects. After years of obscurity "...without masters, without guides, often without books..." Fabre was discovered by literary figures of the stature of Maeterlinck. Now Victor Hugo proclaimed him "the Homer of Insects" and he achieved government recognition and a pension. His acclaim was as profound as had been his neglect during the major part of his lifetime.

As I browsed, I was struck by his poignant lament, "I greatly fear that the peach is offered to me when I am beginning to have no teeth wherewith to eat it!" Yet, amazingly, he never was reduced to rancour in his writing. Although, by the time he acquired his property he feared that time had failed him, he clung to his passion for scientific truth.

Reading on, I began to realize why this man of science had appealed to me when I was a child. He himself declared that, although he hoped to interest philosophers who were studying the profound questions of instinct, he particularly addressed himself to the young in hopes of engaging their interest in natural history. By no means have all his conclusions stood the test of time, but, as Edwin Teale assesses his contribution, "All students of insect behaviour, of comparative psychology, of experimental biology are indebted to him. His harvest of facts is invaluable still."

Fabre deserves to be read and enjoyed as much as ever. His work stands as a testament to what the ordinary person can discover if he or she cares enough to try.

Stargazing

Every time I slip on my coat, grab the binoculars, and head out to do some stargazing, I ask myself again why it took me so long to take the plunge. Three things held me back, I guess, two physical and one a state of mind. Because my heat and energy levels have always been low at night, I've sometimes been reluctant to embark on new ventures then. Besides, the star patterns looked impossibly complex. I'm ashamed to admit it, but I suspect that I also had a superstitious fear that if I learned a rational approach to the stars, they would lose much of their glamour and mysticism. I made the mistake of thinking that the truth would make the stars seem common. I couldn't have been more mistaken.

It took the prompting of two newly interested friends to get Barry and me started one evening early in August. "It's easy," my friend Mare encouraged as we walked out into the splendour of a perfect, moonless night. George pointed his flashlight beam to outline the Big Dipper. Once we had found that, Mare and George patiently pointed out the Little Dipper, Bootes and the Northern Crown. To our delight, we saw them perfectly and picked them out ourselves several times while Mare and George moved off, looking around the sky for more constellations.

When we returned to the house, we were prepared to be converts. We could find our way around a small section of the northwest sky. We had a starting place. We all agreed that it was a fine way for friends to spend an evening together. It's a distinct advantage to have more than one pair of eyes to search for groupings. Star watching combines the fun of a hunt with the special intimacy of being out after dark together.

As soon as we had put together a selection of guidebooks (we found *The Summer Stargazer* by Robert Claiborne particularly helpful and simple), we were ready to make a foray on our own. We soon found complications. That first night on our own, brightness in the southern sky kept us from seeing anything in that quarter. Later, too, the beginnings of Northern Lights obscured our view to the north, but then, who in his right mind would complain about seeing the Northern Lights? When we quit for the night we were confirmed stargazers with four more constellations added to our collection, including one that has become my favourite, Draco, the dragon that snakes between the Big and Little Dippers.

Previously I had resented a cloudy day which gave way to a clear night. What use was a clear night? Now such nights have become a pleasure. We even grudge the growing moon that dims the stars. On our first try we had stayed safely in the northwest but on subsequent space travels we began to inch our way around the constellations near the horizon. "After all," Barry reasoned, "the star positions change so much we'll have to be prepared. Look at Cygnus. By next January it will have moved all the way from the zenith to the northern horizon." Cautiously, checking and rechecking and forming connected triangles, we found our way around. Just as we were ready to quit one night, Barry offered me the binoculars, "Have a look at that dusty-looking mass over there. Look how many stars are concentrated and see how brilliant they are." When we checked our find back in the house, we found, to our jubilation, that we had stumbled onto the open cluster named "The Pleiades", described by Tennyson as "a swarm of fireflies tangled in a silver braid."

There's so much to look forward to now. The relationships will stay the same, but the stars will move around the heavens and new stars will appear for us in the early night as the seasons advance. So far we've just looked for constellations. Ahead of us are planets, and individual stars of special significance like the giant red star Antares. As we use binoculars more and perhaps a telescope, all will be new again. Already Barry is looking into the scientific aspects and is talking in terms of light years, while I am looking over books of myths, searching for the stories behind the names. So far and yet so near: I'm starting to feel as if I hold the heavens in the palm of my hand and I've only just begun.

Whiteness at dusk

It was dusk. All day the heat had burned as searingly as at summer's beginning, but now the August night was closing over the hillside pasture where I was walking. Darkness came earlier now. The days were shrinking and pulling towards fall. As I wandered up the hill, the air at my face was still the light, warm air of summer, but eddies of cool dampness caught at my ankles. Summer had passed the turning point now.

I walked heedlessly for some time in the fading light, letting the wiry stems of Queen Anne's lace whip at my legs. At last, I began to notice the way its swaying white cups floated over the darkening pasture. I picked one and looked at it closely. For all its toughness, the weed had a lovely flower, like the foam of old lace with a black fleck like a bee in its centre.

Halfway up the hill, halfway between summer and autumn, halfway between sunset and moonrise, I wandered on, imagining that I was walking in a starfield, or that the flocks of white pasture flowers were ghosts hovering over the cooling earth. I brushed against another flower and scared up a chalk-white, fur-bodied moth, white on white against the darkening hill, and I began to think about the powers of the colour white.

It was fitting that it was the sum of all colours, for there was something exceptional about it, both more and less than the others. On a summer's day it diminished in comparison with the reds, pinks and yellow, but at evening, they receded and it became a beacon, announcing itself to the varied and secret night-life, like the moth I had just seen.

I remembered other whites I had prized, first in the woodland and then in the garden. Some of the best of woods flowers were white, from the slight foamflower and mitrewort to the snowy trillium petals. In the woods white and fear often seemed to go together, for, just as the Queen Anne's lace drew the moth, so the upturned scut of a doe counterbalanced her camouflage brown, drawing attention wherever she went. An albino, a creature all white through an accident of nature, was always at risk and generally faced an early death. When he was startled, the flicker's white rump also alerted predators. And then there were the whites of leaves up-turned before an approaching storm.

Certainly I associated their warnings with memories of childhood fears. But what of the birches? What place could I find for them in the white web I was weaving? I gave up, pictured their linear beauty against the forest, and went on to think of white in the garden.

I remembered the long nights in drought years when I stood all evening holding a hose over the garden, smelling the dusty earth turning damp and watching the colours fade as the sky faded too. If I was lucky, the woodcock wavered over my head, and the bats swooped and dipped around the barn, searching out insects that the swallows had missed during the day. It was then that whiteness, and the fragrance that so often accompanies it, first came to my mind.

When I first saw the insignificant, greenish-white flowers of nico-tine I had been disappointed. In fact, I had rooted most of the plants out, leaving only a few at the garden's edge. One night, after finishing my watering, I was passing the flowers when I was stopped by an ethereal smell. I looked at the nicotine, now luminous in the dimness, and realized that these flowers were part of a secret night world of which I knew nothing. The white lilacs, roses, peonies, phlox – all came into their own once darkness fell, throwing out an eloquent lure for creatures I never saw.

Back in my pasture, I walked on until the night swallowed even the Queen Anne's lace's brightness. In the eastern woods a screech owl called, another ghost to go with the ghostly flowers that I could no longer see now, but only feel around me. But as I turned and started home, I saw the cold, white light of the moon rising to illu-minate the hillside in a different way.

Reunion

All evening the conversation had been hectic and superficial. We had not seen my friend Anne and her husband Dick for five years.

On their way East for their first holiday alone since the birth of their children, they were spending a night with us. We were filling in the gaps between the compressed news of Christmas letters and making links with the past when Anne and I had been to university together. Five years of life do not unfold easily, though, and the stories of difficult births, lonely times, feeling our way through jobs, parents getting older, but still the same, were told in low relief.

Our boys went up to bed and still we sat around the long pine table in our kitchen, but now the talk became less guarded and filled with a lurking bitterness. Wasn't it strange, remarked Anne, that a man who was always prompt for his job could never get home on time to look after his child when he knew his wife had to go to work. Wasn't it remarkable that a man who had an M.A. and was widely respected was unable to master the rudiments of cooking.

Well, that, Dick said, was precisely what marriage seemed to be about. Women could never let anything go. Just one time forget something and you never heard the end of it. As for cooking, he didn't have time to learn cooking. He had important work he had to do. The red flag of "women's work" hovered on his lips but remained unsaid.

Robert Frost's "trial by existence" had been hard for the two of them, harder than any of us could have imagined back in university. Anne had become stronger; Dick had grown in understanding. But the price, we began to see, was too high. This holiday was not a joyous reunion for the two of them. It was a last try to keep a marriage together where all the pain and confusion of coping with a handicapped child had spilled like acid on their love.

At last the talk ran down and we sat listening to the moths hitting the screen. "Why don't we go out and see what their stars look like," Dick suggested. "They should be pretty good out here away from the lights." Barry and Dick got up and went out and Anne and I followed more slowly.

"I feel so confused and afraid," Anne told me as I closed the screen door behind us. "There are no guideposts here. No one can help us. There's not a lot left, but neither of us seems to be able to do much about it. There are too many bad memories. I feel like we're slipping farther apart every day and there's no time and no way to say 'Stop. This is all wrong. We still do love each other.'"

Far across the field a great horned owl called. The night was clear and moonless and the stars and fireflies seemed to unite to swim around our heads. Vega, Boötes, Corona Borealis: we found all the major constellations of the late summer sky and then sat down on the porch to enjoy the flow of the Milky Way. "Did you know Indians thought that was the path of the spirits ascending to heaven?" asked Dick.

Outside in the starlight there was no place for the pettiness of the kitchen. The distances of the stars we were considering made a scale too great for human passions. Even our faces were remote in the pale light. The resentment that had flared in the kitchen seemed pointless. A cold little wind, speaking of the coming of fall, brushed past us. On opposite sides of the nearest field we heard a pair of foxes barking. From the sound of the barks they were moving quickly, but as they travelled they kept up a perfect linkage, a call and an answer, until we could hear their voices no longer. Finally Barry and I went in, leaving Anne and Dick sitting wordlessly watching the stars go west.

They left early the next morning, quietly and with none of the fanfare of a honeymoon. I will not hear from them until next Christmas: "We are fine. I got a promotion. Dick has been teaching the older grades this fall. Suzanne is taking skating now." I hope they make it.

Where cardinal flowers grow

Very rarely, the elements of many different areas combine in one small place to make an island, a meeting place for an unusually rich variety of species. One August evening, attracted by the vivid red of cardinal flowers, we came on such a place by accident. When we stopped to admire these uncommon flowers, we discovered that within a stone's throw grew more different types of wildflowers than we had ever seen together. What brought these flowers together? Within the space of two acres we found a woods sheltered by a hill and a tiny marsh through which trickled a stream that then went on to flow under the road and through a more open woods. Added to this was a small enclosed meadow growing thickly with black-eyed Susans.

The radiance of that August evening stays with me. First of all there were the cardinal flowers, the reddest red there is, blazing against a jungle background of dark green August foliage. Their red reflected into the purling stream that passed beside them, headed for the nearby lake. Not only was this place a haven for many varieties; the season's turning brought together the last samples of summer with the first flowers of fall, greatly adding to the diversity.

High in the treetops, where the sun still lingered, a gusty south wind was blowing, yet in the little swamp before us the few remaining orange jewelweed flowers barely moved. Hidden in the grass at the meadow's edge we found one last buttercup, as welcome as a drift of them in July. Also at the meadow's edge stood milkweeds, their scent heavy in the falling dew. A few butterflies still hung from the clusters of dusty flowers. Here all was summer.

Yet only a little farther down the road we found the first goldenrod, its greenish-yellow flowers barely open, and alongside the fluffy pink of summery joe-pyeweed, we saw the first pale asters of fall. Binding together all these flowers of summer and fall, woods and swamp, trailed the creamy froth of virgin's bower.

We had chanced upon a perfect environment, and for some years we returned to see the cardinal flowers, the only group of them of which we knew, and to try to better our record for the number of different wildflowers we could find blooming on the same day. Each year we played the game more diligently, grasping at a single white clover blossom to add to the purple, yellow and pink kinds, or a scruffy, half-dead dandelion to boost our total. Each year the place seemed more like a secret island, near a lake and its cottages, yet innocent of their influence.

I'd like to be able to say, as sundials often do, "I count only the sunlit hours". I'd like to think of this wild and secret garden blooming undisturbed each summer, but last year we arrived to find that change had come to our oasis. In the field of black-eyed Susans sat two trailers, roughing it, with all the paraphernalia that they seem to require, including the blaring radio – apparently essential to outdoor life.

We hesitated, all our expectant pleasure extinguished. We felt like intruders. A wavering blue light in a trailer window suggested that the occupants were busy with television, and, we reasoned, wouldn't be disturbed by us. We decided that since we had come to count we would do so, and perfunctorily we worked our way, one along each side of the road, finding here a late vervain, with only a few tiny purple florets remaining on its wiry stems, and there among the gravel the slight candles of plantain. No birds competed with the radio.

Our half-hearted count yielded as choice a selection of species as always, but we knew this was the last summer we would visit our secret place. At last we reached the mossy little brook where once the cardinal flowers flourished. The banks were trampled down and crumbling into the water: a solitary, broken, red-flowered spire quavered in the passing current. To the tune of "You are my Sunshine" we turned away and walked slowly back to our car.

Horsetails

It's funny the way some plants follow you through life. I'm not talking about the rare and the beautiful. It's the metaphor plants I'm thinking of – the unusual ones that crop up in all kinds of circumstances throughout life. The common horsetail has become such a one for me. Over the years I've looked at it upside down and inside out and yet I'm always discovering new and interesting things about this homely plant.

I began picking joint grass, as I called it, as soon as I was able to pick anything. There was something about the decisive snap as the segments pulled apart that made it as attractive a toy as dandelions and more reliable. No telltale sticky mess remained to annoy parents when I snapped and piled horsetail segments. When I went to school, I took horsetails with me. I'd graduated from taking apart now and I found that refitting the precise joints of the wiry plant, was even more satisfying. All the way to school I refitted spires of joint grass and then saved them in my pockets as a promise that I really would get free and return home later in the day.

One day when I was eight I saw a picture of dinosaurs posing beneath (how remarkable) towering horsetails, read further and learned that my joint grass came from a family that had been on earth for more than three hundred and fifty million years. That afternoon I returned to the horsetail patch and deliberately shrank until I became a grasshopper looking up at a horsetail jungle.

As an adult I keep running into the common horsetail, and, of course, each encounter adds to its associations. Recently I've read that the queer, rough surface I used to finger all the way to school contains glassy crystals. Because of this, the plants were once used for scouring dirty dishes. Now I know the origins of one of my old friend's names, "scouring rush".

In my reading I've learned that the horsetail is a distant relative of ferns and club mosses. Because it has an underground stem or rhizome that branches through the soil and throws up new stems, it is difficult to eradicate, and has none of the fern's popularity. I've never known this spreading to be a problem, though, because I've always met it by roadsides or railroad tracks, where its short growth could do no harm.

I've found the mechanics of the plant to be interesting too. Above ground there are two kinds of shoots to watch out for, so different that it's hard to believe they are attached to the same plant. The sterile shoot has whorls of plumy greenery, but more notable is the straight brown fertile shoot with its rings of scaly leaves and a spore cone for its tip. To see these unmistakeable shoots is to be convinced of their prehistoric connections.

The reproductive story of the spores is complicated but the spores themselves have a special interest which is worth relating. Unlike those of ferns, they are green, short-lived and hence vulnerable. Each has four moisture-sensitive straps attached to it. As the dampness of the air varies, these straps coil and uncoil like microscopic springs to help scatter the spores and ensure that the plant continues.

My favourite memory of the gawky horsetail concerns passing on some of my enthusiasm for it. While working on an Ontario Arts Council textile project with a local school, I planned a lesson using native dye plants. What dyestuff could be more natural to use than the common, easily accessible horsetail? One by one, my groups of ten children filed down to the school kitchen with me and we made a liquor out of the plant that had lived when dinosaurs were around. Eagerly, the children immersed their miniature skeins of white wool and waited. With each group the results were the same. From the stems of the drab roadside plant came something wonderful. What the children drew forth was yarn of a soft, stone green. Magic from prehistory.

Goodbye to the land

There is a sense that goes beyond reason that some places are home, while others, no matter how much they offer, never evoke the longing for rootedness. Never had I felt closer to being home than during those years when I lived on the long and winding road that stretched past Blue Ridge Farm. And tomorrow I had to leave with no real hope of ever returning there to live.

It was dusk and I was walking with my friends Clayton and Gail on their father's farm, looking for the small herd of cows he was building. That was our spoken purpose, but I was saying goodbye to the land I had come to love.

I looked long and painfully over the farm. To the west were the woods where in a clearing the bees would be returning to their hives for the night, the first bees I had ever known. To think that next winter I would not be able to stoop to the hives and listen for the secret wellbeing hidden inside.

We walked in the shadow of the ridge and looked at the slope where the sugar bush was sheltered, the bush where Barry had carried brimming sap pails for the first time. Next year our friends would sit tending the fire and telling stories but Barry and I would not be there.

We passed the sand pit where the cliff swallows flew and the bank where the family had been finding fossils for one hundred and fifty years. I shook my head, dazzled with the pain of leaving, and reflected on the surprising obedience of heart to will that would place us in a plane tomorrow.

The setting sun seemed to recede before our feet as we walked slowly across the fields below the ridge, Clayton silent and his little five year old sister, Gail, chattering like a robin. Here was the field where last July we had helped in the rush to get the grain stooks piled before a thunderstorm. How could it be that I was leaving this place where I belonged?

In the bottom pasture we found the cows, a family herd, carefully built with much sacrifice, and we sat a while on a rock pile, reminiscing about the characters in the herd, until the dew and the first stars reminded us that we were expected back home.

Now Gail, who had insisted on coming with us, looked at the long distance back to the farmhouse lights and begged to be carried. At first we took turns shouldering her for the distance of a field, but in the end Clayton stretched his tired back and said she would have to get home on her own steam. "And how am I supposed to do that?" she demanded plaintively. Clayton sighed and looked over at me. "I guess you'll have to do it by putting one foot in front of the other all the way until we get back home," he answered.

One foot in front of the other. We left the next day, and it's been like that ever since for us on the road back home.

I always assumed that I would establish a new home of my own, a place to which I could cling with unshakeable roots for the rest of my life. When I came to the Blue Ridge Farm concession to live, I thought I had found it. But reality, something with which I've never been at home, intervened, and cast Barry and me as wanderers for ten years. Never again did we find a place where roots were possible. How many these days do?

As we moved, I clung to an image of beloved trees, fields and a house, but sometimes it flashed out at me that home was within me and for always, not a place, but a state of mind. If I took my steps lightly and with love and appreciation, wherever they might lead me, I was there already.

I'm still walking towards home, one step in front of the other, only now I'm not so sure what it looks like any more, and I'm surprised to find I don't care. As far as the journey back home goes, I'm beginning to think the getting there is all.

Autumn

Quinte revisited

When I think of Quinte I think of light. I see the light that comes off its lakes and bays; I see the light of its big skies and the light that shines on its fields. Quinte, for me, is one of the magic places. Visits there were the highpoints of many summers when I was growing up.

But it had been many years since I had returned, and as September approached this year, I knew I wanted to go back to steal a look at all the places I'd loved. I wanted, too, to see my boys discovering its high spots before they were grown up. "Your father was so sad the last time we went to Lake on the Mountain," my mother had said to me recently. "It seemed like a waste being there without you girls."

Part of me said it was better not to go. Memories were meant to be left as such. Now that a bridge had replaced the Deseronto ferry, Prince Edward County and its white sand beaches would be all too vulnerable to an excess of tourists. Many things would have changed, I knew. Twenty years ago we had driven along back roads so isolated that families had rushed from their shanties to stare at a passing car. Then my parents had sketched outside many a handsome abandoned settler's house while my sister and I had explored, discovering beautiful turning of stair posts and quaint wallpapers. If I went back now, would the losses be too great? Would I wish I never had returned?

We crossed on the Glenora ferry in a swirl of late September rain. Never before had I been able to come to Quinte in the off-season. Jeremy and I stood in the cold, pelting rain and watched the stone buildings of the opposite dock draw closer to the ferry and I could feel that he sensed the adventure ahead.

As we drove past gentle forests and fields of golden pumpkins, always catching glimpses of water that sparkled now that the shower had passed, I knew I had been right to come. There had been changes, but Quinte had not changed. There were unsightly trailer parks packed between century farms at East and West Lakes, but, on the other hand, there, after twenty years, was my favourite vegetable stand, resplendent with squashes and bunches of late gladiolas.

And then we were at our rented cottage and once again I was looking across at the sweeping crescent beach of the provincial park, listening and listening and listening to the waves of Lake Ontario racing in to our own pebbly beach. Leaving the car still packed, the boys and I crossed the stony shore. Yes, you still could find fossils here, I told them, triumphantly holding up a petrified snail shell.

In the primitive cottage that evening, I looked at the lakelight glittering outside our window and wavering on the cottage's varnished ceiling. Far down the beach, two boys, made small again by distance, skipped stones and gestured at the broad sky. Later that night, I could barely sleep for wanting to watch the moon's passage across the lake.

The next morning and the next we flew around the small "island", rediscovering all its variety. There was hill country and the flat "country of the pointed firs". We passed the fields where dried spires told me that in summer blue weed still mirrors the blue of the bays far below.

At Lake on the Mountain, while the boys went from the view of the ferries passing far below to the queer little lake sheltered by willows, I stood in front of the red brick building that was formerly a hotel. One hot summer night long ago I'd listened to the clank-clank of cars rolling off the ferry, counting the time by their passage. Now, below me, the sound was unchanged.

On the last morning, entirely alone, we padded far across the sand dunes while I told my boys stories I had once been told of rolling sand that buried fences and even houses.

That afternoon, I looked over my shoulder one last time at old stone walls and at apple orchards sloping to the lake, and at gulls flying inland past the pines to the cornfields. I looked again and they were gone. Gone, but with great happiness I knew that they remained unchanged.

No time to lose

No time to lose. No time, no time, no time. It was one of those days when I heard it everywhere. Worst of all, I heard time pounding at my heels. Frustration twisted within me until, in despair, I headed out to my favourite bare patch of granite to sort things out.

I couldn't reduce my schedule. I hashed and rehashed the have-to's. The knot tightened and I paced back and forth, trying to shake off my mood, muttering to myself about needing two lives to get done half of what I needed and wanted to do.

Gradually, I tired and sat down. Slowly, a natural time set in, replacing the turbulence within me. I noticed I was absently running my fingers over the glacial scars that gouged my pink granite seat. Here, I thought, was time on a different scale. These rocks had been scraped and rounded by a weight of time beyond anything I could grasp.

Having slowed my thoughts, and let myself dabble with the notion of eons, I let myself go a little farther and realized how fine it was just to be sitting on granite on a warm autumn day, letting my fingers trace all the marks and messages I found on the rocks.

But I couldn't change that easily. In ten more minutes I would need to pick up Morgan from his piano lesson and hurry home to get supper so Barry could get off to his meeting. Perhaps later while I darned socks and stitched on buttons I could start working out my points for the article due on Friday (if nobody phoned, that was). Still, the sun and the contact with the age-old rocks was too much for me. I simply couldn't begin to fetch back my earlier desperation.

I tried to think of what was lacking in the path of my days. I re-made resolutions. I promised myself to leave the dusting, even if that did mean braving the contempt of some of my friends. In its place I would try harder to keep the loom threaded so I would not be saddened when I passed its reproachful emptiness. Somehow I would work out a compromise between good practising and giving up so I could still enjoy playing the piano on the few evenings I could manage it. I wanted to keep having friends over without worrying about whether the house was tidy or the food was elegant.

All the time I was planning, I was aware that filling my days was not a good answer to the pressure I felt. Time should be counted in terms of love and attention.

I thought about what really mattered and I knew I already had all I needed. I remembered watching Morgan walk towards us from the plane after he'd spent two weeks in Philadelphia. Could this poised, shiny-faced teenager really be my son? I thought of Jeremy's bright eyes as he showed me his latest treasure, salvaged from the dump. ("The motor still works, Mom", and I, who am not in the least mechanical, suddenly quite saw the fascination.) I thought of the intensely satisfying wordless walks with Barry in which somehow everything that ever needs to be said is. I remembered how rich I'd felt in being able to talk for hours with a friend whose father had just died, sharing her sorrow. This was reality, and it was all around me, yet it was slipping by me, not because I had too little time, but because I paid too little attention.

It was attentiveness that could defeat time. A hectic day was not lost if I had truly looked at my aunt's beautiful smile. I wanted to be sure I'd really seen it, so it would stay with me. It was important to hear all the different tones in the call of the wild geese as they flew over while I hung clothes.

I rose to get the car. Just then a breeze brought me the scent of pine sap and I drank it in, reminding myself that soon the cold weather would rob the air of scents. Really, my problem was not a question of too little time, but of too much that was worthwhile, and I wasn't going to wish that otherwise.

Pond succession

When I reached the long, broad pond at the back of the property I stopped in surprise, for half the pond was nearly gone. Where deep water had stretched for many more than the eight years during which we had visited it, there was now only a pond of green reeds and rushes that had grown up to hide and absorb the water. To my casual eyes the pond had always been much the same. Animals, plants and birds changed somewhat from season to season, but always the pond looked about the way it had when I first saw it. Now, though, half of it was choked with cattails and no longer had enough open water to reflect the sky. Once again I was faced with the mutability of nature.

I sat down on a rounded, bare lookout rock. Over the brief years that I had been coming here the pond had become a marsh and I had not noticed the signs that it was happening. If I looked at my memories of it, perhaps I could piece together the transition.

Five years ago the bleached trunks of many drowned trees had stretched up out of the water. In winter the wind used to hit those trees and pile blowing snow in drifts. The last few years, though, most of them had fallen below the surface, leaving a long, smooth stretch of openness where the wind packed the snow, making a fine, fast surface for cross country skiing. The pond must have been old for them to have fallen in. During the process their decaying debris must have built good mud on the bottom to encourage the growth of the plants that had now choked its water.

Over the water that remained at the far end of the pond came shivers of wind, a rain-laden wind that I knew would bring a change from the uncommonly sultry weather of the past week. Down at this end I saw three black ducks swimming. The leader, teased by a red-bodied dragonfly, turned his head. He caught sight of me on my rock and splashed into flight, taking the other two with him. At the rate things were going, after a few more summers there would not be enough water here for ducks.

How could it be that this pond of living water was changing to a pond of grass? I remembered now that some of the tree stumps had supported a few ferns and tufts of grass, good holding places for soil, and, yes, that stand of cattails had always been on the far side of the pond, only now it stretched across to my side too.

The wind rose again and a scattering of leaves blew across the marsh from the nearby woods. For years these leaves and dying water vegetation had nourished and filled in the pond floor to quicken a new kind of life that was coming. In time the ducks would be leaving and so would the beaver whose channel cut through the pickerel weeds near the shore. But other life would fill the marsh. Already, secure among the cattails, I could see conical muskrat houses.

As the plants took up more water, and as their decay made the depths shallow, the pond would become a lush meadow, and then would come the first saplings, and then... As always, the chain goes on without end.

I looked at the arrowhead leaves swaying in the slight currents close to my shore, and further back to the solid mass of cattails and bur reeds. I didn't want to see the pond end, and with it the fascinating world it supported, yet how right it was that it had gathered its richness together to bring forth another state.

Now, though, I was faced with more immediate changes. For some time I had heard thunder in the distance. A sudden peal shook the rock on which I sat and the cold rain, which had been heavy in the air all afternoon, poured over me in sheets. I headed home cold but exhilarated. After all, change was the guarantee that life itself would continue.

The harp of wind

"Pull that old rug over you if you're cold," the old man suggested. We were sitting together on a steamer trunk at the last auction of the year. "See that box over there? There's more in that than you would think. I lived in this house when I was a young lad and I remember all the things for sale here. In that box is a zither that used to belong to my mother." A gust of rainy wind shook down yellow leaves around us.

"My Mother loved that zither. It was the only present my Dad ever gave her. We didn't have any money then, and he didn't care much about anything fancy anyhow. Mother'd been a teacher and she loved music. She was always looking at those parlour organs with all the fretwork on them.

"One year near Christmas, Dad got a bit extra somehow and he went into town and bought her that zither and brought it home. My, how she loved the thing and us kids loved it too. She used to play it like it really was a harp. To us it sounded better than one of them organs, even – all light and sparkly, until you just had to be happy and sing with it too. Any song you'd want she could play.

"Nights after she'd put us to bed, and Dad was sitting asleep by the stove, she'd turn down the lamp and sit by the dark window and play just for herself. She didn't play songs then. No. I've never heard anything like it, but I've never forgotten it neither. It was like killdeers over the fields in spring, and the rain in the churchyard where her baby was buried, and like she was a girl again.

"One day, in March, I think it was, a pedlar came round. Mother couldn't buy much, but she told him she'd take a few things and she gave him a bowl of soup. He saw her zither and asked her about it. She played a bit for him and then she went upstairs to get the money she owed him. When she came down again he was gone. That night when she sat down to play she found he'd taken her zither with him.

"I listened on the stairs. Father was sorry, but when he felt bad he got cross and he told her she'd been foolish and there'd not be another harp like that for her. Mother didn't say a word, but I heard her walking and walking over the rag carpets in the front room, long after he went to bed.

"The funny thing was, two weeks later, the zither was found. A neighbour found it tossed in a dry ditch three concessions over. It was as good as ever and we thought Mother'd be glad to have it back. But d'you know, she wasn't. She took it and put it away in the attic and she never touched it again – wouldn't let us have it neither. Being young, I thought she was heartless. Sometimes, too, I thought maybe all that music she'd loved so much was still locked away in the box and wanting to get out. Afterwards, I knew how she felt and I was sorry." The old man turned away and fretted the yellow leaves on the chest beside him.

Just a half hour later I found I was leaving the sale with a dusty, dove-tailed box whose contents I had not yet been able to examine because of the press of the crowd. Before I reached the car, I set the box on the ground and drew out the zither. Even if I couldn't play it, it would make a lovely ornament, this small harp, with its amber finish and gilt decorations as bright as when the old man's mother had played it. I touched a string and the noise was ripe and only slightly metallic. I stopped the string like a violin and the pitch rose, reedy but beautiful. Then I stroked across the long untouched strings and I imagined I heard the killdeer's song and the rain in it. I played on with the strings telling me what to do with them and I thought I heard the mother's song that had been locked away for so long.

Dye plants

Walnuts and goldenrod and lichens and sumac. Mushrooms and willow and oak galls and bracken. These are among the delights of an autumn forage for dyestuffs. I have to admit I seldom get to use many of them in any one year any more. Still, I feel I know each one better because of my dyeing adventures. Simply seeing a dyeplant that I have used brightens the walk on which I encounter it.

Take goldenrod, the first plant I used for natural dyeing experiments some years ago. Two-year-old Morgan and I set out for a vacant lot at the end of the town in which we were living at that time to harvest great armloads of the bright flowers. It was such a gay, carefree feeling to come on a flower growing wild in such profusion that we could safely gather quantities of it. As we lugged our spoils cheerfully home, I remember people stared in disbelief at the new teacher's crazy wife. What would she ever do with a weed like that? I could have pointed out that in England some goldenrods are prized garden flowers, but I doubt that they would have believed me. Anyhow, Morgan and I held our heads up and brought home our flowery spoils.

That afternoon we spent a happy hour pulling the flowers apart out on our lawn. Then I tipped them into an old preserving kettle with rainwater I had collected during a recent storm. Next came the brewing to draw out the dye, a process which varies in pleasantness according to the odour of the dyestuff. In the case of this, my first experiment, the house filled with a pungent, ferny scent. After several hours of steeping the flowers, I strained them out, leaving a murky, brown liquor which made me very doubtful about prospective results. I looked at my creamy skeins of wool, carefully pretreated with alum to help them absorb the colour better, held my breath, and plunged them into the hot dyebath.

I was lucky to have chosen goldenrod for my first venture. The colour began to bloom through the wool quickly, a satisfying experience that made me impatient for the necessary hour's simmering to be up. At last I carefully lifted my skeins out to admire. The common goldenrod flowers had yielded a clear, brassy yellow.

Unfortunately I did not realize that many natural dyes are not colourfast and hung my skeins in my weaving room by a window where their bright colour cheered many winter days for me with memories of my foraging expedition. By spring the yellow had lost its liveliness, but by then I was looking forward to new adventures.

All summer I simmered pots of dye until my family complained loudly about the strange smells. Often my clothesline was festooned with skeins of green, brown, gold or yellow wool. I began looking at my surrounding plants with eyes not just appreciative, but covetous, too.

I was happy with the colours I achieved, soft, one-of-a kind shades that harmonized beautifully with each other. I began to prize my bits of hand-dyed wool and to use them for special projects just as pioneer women had been able to colour only the best of their possessions.

Because I lived far from stores that carried assortments of coloured wool, it was most convenient for me to keep a few pounds of white wool to dye myself as it was needed. In this way, when I wanted a contrasting colour for the leaping horse on Morgan's new sweater, I collected a handful of lichens and soon had a bronze that made the horse stand out perfectly.

The dyeing adventure has become a continuing pleasure. As do other enthusiasts, I've become interested enough that I've extended my season with the use of such things as onion skins (an excellent dyestuff that produces a lively, warm brown for me), and carrot tops (that give a surprisingly clear, pale yellow), but, best of all, I enjoy the excuse dyeing gives me in the warmer months, to be out of doors, searching, studying and dreaming.

If you go harvesting, please remember to respect your dye plants and never exhaust your supply. Some are very rare, and some, like lichens, need hundreds of years to mature.

Sanctuary

Once a stranger sought sanctuary at Foley Mountain. He came asking nothing, but in the scheme of things, nothing turned out to be too much.

I was returning with Morgan from nursery school late on an October day when I saw a man stooped, blowing on a fire. It was queer that he apparently had no car and yet was lingering close to nightfall. People aren't allowed in the park after sunset. Still, he could have been one of the exceptions who was allowed a night's camping while hiking the Rideau Trail. Then, I forgot about him.

The next afternoon and the next, Morgan and I saw him again, nursing a fire or sitting on a picnic table gazing at the woods. The third day, a Friday, he stared at me in an odd, expressive way, quite unlike that of the usual park visitors. He looked with a mixture of defiance and pleading and then slipped off the table and walked towards the woods with the brittle steps of someone tremendously hurt.

I didn't see the stranger over the weekend, but Monday he was back in the clearing again and this time I became afraid. As I drove around the curve I saw him lunge after a squirrel with a hunting knife. More than the knife, it was the fierce gesture that made me afraid. Yet, when he saw me, he froze and once again his eyes tugged at mine as if he and not the squirrel, were the prey.

I had to tell Barry. With two young children to protect I had no choice. Still, while I waited for him to return from questioning the stranger, I couldn't stop seeing the troubled eyes. "You're right. He is different," Barry said when he returned. "I wouldn't be surprised if he is a bit unbalanced. Harmless enough, though, I should think. He's working in town and he was camping. When I told him he couldn't camp here he said he would go to the campground across town. But he said he still wanted to come here after work until dark, and there's nothing I can do about that." Torn between the knife and the eyes, I said nothing. Unasked, a stranger was sharing my home ground. Was he ruthless and dangerous or just another loner like I me who, if confronted with grief, would always head for the woods?

For some time, the man avoided us. Occasionally I saw him sitting staring into the woods, holding on hard, I should have imagined from his attitude. One day he moved slowly towards the car and motioned me to stop. I cranked the window down an inch. "I just wanted to know if you had a light," he said. For no good reason I was reminded of a stray dog casing a family for a home. Of course I had no light to give him and no words either. I had stopped, but I was afraid. It was too late now to push the door locks. Women can't afford to trust, I reminded myself, and I shook my head, smiled a tight smile, resealed the window and drove off.

I didn't see the stranger again. Soon after, Barry, out on a night patrol, saw the glow of a fire. As it happened, two police officers were parked up the road doing paper work. He asked them to come with him and evict the man. As a routine, they put his name through the computer and found out: the man standing in mute misery by his fire was on parole from B.C., where he had been doing time for wounding an officer with a knife. It was over then, Barry told me later. The police had driven him to the public campground and warned him to stay away from Foley Mountain. Before he got in the car he had cast Barry a look of despair at the betrayal.

In town, people told us how our stranger stayed on alone at the campground until the deep snow came. Then he disappeared. They laughed at his foolishness in camping out in our winter. But I knew that because of prudence and duty we had failed him. He had come here, deeply wounded, to seek sanctuary, clinging to a pitiful dream of self-reliance. Perhaps he had hoped that somewhere, someone wouldn't turn him down, but prudence and duty had left him without hope.

Apple-stealing time

Recalling stealing apples on a wild, free evening after school, I am reminded of a golden age. Just as the late autumn light has a special brightness to it, there was a quality of strength, daring and freedom to those days that I think is forgotten later. In some ways, the time of apple raids was a last stand before puberty closed some doors and opened new ones.

Already by four o'clock there were long shadows as we slunk past the neighbours' houses to the end of the road where Hisey's orchard stood. There were five of us lanky eleven-year-olds and Nancy's little sister Lynnie, along on sufferance by her mother's orders. We made it safely past Old Lady Andrews' house and for once she didn't pop out like the witch in a toy weather forecasting house. Once we reached the old orchard we could not be seen and could run as openly as we wanted. We always ran in those days, although not out of haste – ran and loped and cantered. It seemed the wind-blown grass was running in sympathy and even the crows who flew up from their apple raids were blown off in the wind.

I found an old ladder lying woven into the bleached grass and balanced along it until, "crack", a rung broke and I made an exaggerated jump that sent the others shrieking off. We squished through the cidery-smelling piles of rotten apples and Nancy picked one up and pitched it at a tree where it burst and oozed down the trunk.

But we were there for apples, and, watching the fading light, we hunched over and began our gleaning. We'd set out to take windfalls. Mothers rarely objected if you could tell them you had left the trees untouched. Also, there was a special savour to hunting the secret apples hidden in the grass. Our shopping bags were nearly full when Nancy, lured by a fat apple high in a tree, scrambled up, seized it and tossed first it, and then others down to us. But how could we carry them? Giggling out of all proportion with the situation, we began stuffing them under our shirts. We strutted around shaking our chests until they heaved and rolled.

At last Jane shook her hair out of her face and said, "Another few years and we won't be able to do this any more."

"What do you mean?" I asked.

"We'll have to wear bras," she said baldly. "And anyway, I guess we'll be too fancy to come down here and steal apples."

We all grew sober. Life was fine just the way it was. Who would ever want bumps on your chest? They'd only get in the way. Besides, that was only the start of it. The big girls couldn't run any more just for the fun of it. I minced around the trees pretending to wear high heels. "That's how they walk," I said, contemptuously.

"Yeah, and you can bet they never throw rotten apples," said Marbeth, kicking at an apple pile.

"Being grown up is no good at all," said Jane. "All those girls ever think about is boys, and you'd have to be out of your mind to want anything to do with them. All they ever do is wreck things. Look at that fort we dug and they caved it in for nothing. We never even bothered them."

"Yeah, who'd want to?" said Lorna.

I don't know if we said we wouldn't let it happen, but in the clear, cold time of apple-stealing, I'm sure we thought we could escape. We would be too smart ever to fall into a trap like growing up.

The dew had fallen without our noticing it and the orchard was wetter and colder than we had thought. "Nancee," whined Lynnie, "the street lights have been on for ages, and you know Mommy said we'd get it if we weren't home by then. 'Sides, you were climbing again and you know she said girls aren't supposed to."

We straightened our lithe, skinny bodies and arched our chests to feel the apple plunder shift and bounce as we prepared to negotiate the side street again. "Saturday we should come back again when we've got all day," said Jen. But we never did.

Dear Jack letter

Dear Jack, (I'll call you that, although I have no idea what your real name is.):

It's been two weeks now since you pedalled up to the park with two young raccoons in a cardboard box, spilled them out of the box and left.

I'm sure you aren't very interested in what happened to them after you left, Jack. After all, you were able to leave them without any apparent thought for their welfare. But, you see, Jack, for Barry and me there is a litany of sadness each fall as we see the pets of summer abandoned in the park. "Somebody will take care of her." "He'll find another home," think the well-meaning. Some simply don't care. Once a cheery Grade 4 class on a hike with Barry found a heaving, tightly-secured burlap bag deep in the woods. When Barry cut open the bag the children were shocked to see four kittens that had been left to die of starvation.

But one way or another, they all do die, or, in the case of those who do manage to adapt and survive, they prey unproportionately on the wild creatures who live here naturally. We are watching a real decrease in birds such as woodcocks because of the wild cats who skulk in our wetlands in summer and in winter our bird feeders are threatened by them.

When I saw the coons I could keep silent no longer, probably because, of all the animals that have been dumped here, they were the most affectionate. Let's face it, Jack, an animal who has been domesticated is a cripple. You taught these creatures to love you and then betrayed them.

On your bicycle trip into the park did you stop to think about the fate of the two coons after you turned your back on them? Like it or not, this is how the story continued.

You didn't know it, Jack, but our biology student Marc saw you discard the raccoons and warned us that they were in the Conservation Area. That weekend the coons, too friendly for their own good, waddled up to park visitors and clambered over cars, seeking food and attention. For the most part, in return they got suspicion and alarm. Some people even stopped in at the house to see if we knew there were two rabid raccoons attacking cars and terrifying children.

As I said, a pet confronting the wild is a cripple, a wild pet as well as a tame one. As the Adamsons and many others have shown, a wild pet can only be released with painstaking long-term commitment. Domestic pets, on the other hand, which do not belong to the natural balance, should never be released for the sake of the indigenous wild animals that may not survive their predation.

Did you stop at all to wonder how your pets would cope,

dropped in an unfamiliar area, with no knowledge of sanctuaries and access to food? The park, with its garbage cans of food, is usually oversupplied with raccoons, which now at summer's end would be facing a cutback in this food and fighting viciously amongst themselves. I've seen a bull raccoon fight, Jack, and it's a memorable experience. Fall brings the hunting season. Soon now we will be hearing the ungodly row of coon hounds in the middle of the night. How do you think these trusting little ones will make out?

Over years of hard experience we've learned that cats, the full-grown ones, at least, soon learn to be wary of people, particularly official-looking people, but this pair of coons must have really loved you, Jack. When, no longer able to ignore the problem, Barry rolled up in the truck Sunday after work, the two climbed willingly into the cab with him and cuddled up together in his lap. Would you understand how sick he felt then?

There was no hope of finding a suitable home for the animals, so, reluctantly, Barry drove them to an isolated area where there was a slim chance they might be able to fend for themselves. It was not something he would have done for a domestic animal.

The week after Barry pried the reluctant raccoons from his knee and closed the door on them, you may remember that the September rains began and every day was cold and wet.

(Sincerely, etc.)

Disposable love: it's in the air these days and no one knows where it will end.

Wild harvest

In October it is hard to escape the idea of harvest and storage. In the fall my urge to gather is so strong that I suspect it goes back to a primitive consciousness. Even long after the last of the tomatoes are put away, I cannot walk here without seeing harvest everywhere, from the mushroom caps of chipmunks and the pine-cone midden heaps of the red squirrels to my own more frivolous gatherings.

I have only to hear the rustle of cattails and I'm away. "Green grow the rushes, ho". It would be enough just to watch their waving and think of ancestors slashing armloads to mat their floors. Indians, I've read, used cattail down in blankets, and once, just to see what would happen, I plucked and carded and spun the fluff. The little skein I finished with, cottony to feel, held a surprising warmth.

I would never have gone on, though, as a friend once did, to capture milkweed down in a blanket. It was an act of extravagance, I thought, and yet... She watched the first, silken seed carriers take to the air, she stretched grey woollen warp strings on her loom and she went out in the fields to husk the pods, and winnow the seeds and stuff the remaining silk in her bags. Sometimes I caught her holding the parachutes up for the sun to catch. I heard and saw her rustling her way among the wiry milkweed stalks, surrounded by airborne seeds. On rainy nights although not a spinner, she took the silk between her hands, rolling and stretching it to a ragged rope, and then coiling it in baskets by her loom. When the first snow fell, she sat at her loom and threaded the improbable yarn through her warp threads. The clash of her treadles sounded as true as it would have for a more likely yarn. At Christmas she cut her harvest from the loom and shook it out for both of us to see, a supple, ash-coloured blanket that rippled in firelight. This is what harvest time can lead to.

I pass wild grapes on my walk along the road. Do my boys know they are here, I wonder? The fox whose scats I see farther down the road might find them useful. Grapes and jelly and wine, even purple dye – I search for a purpose for them, knowing full well that they are too few for my plans. I try to remember too, that they are fine to admire with no purpose in mind. The pinning of use to things is irresistible in fall, however, and I move on to the grapes' vines. A few of these could be twined to make a basket, a stout, rough basket. I might even put them to a less practical use. I'd seen geese statues I'd liked shaped of vines bound together.

Also beautiful are the freshly opened orange bittersweet berries I find next, and I make a note to cut some for the house. It was time, too, to gather big bunches of dried weeds to stand in crocks at home against the season when all outdoor weeds were snowbound. And is this the year to collect the fragrant, freshly fallen pine needles and stuff them in a pillow? If I do, will they keep their scent like the pillows you find in old cottages labelled "I pine for you and balsam too"?

I cut back through the deer management area where last summer's thinning to provide this winter's food had left piles of brush and poles. One fall when she was a girl, my sister had made a teepee out of similar poles. It had worked well and had still been standing when we left home. I remember sitting in its shelter watching early snowfalls. You couldn't have anything more useful than poles. I could use them for beans, a summer house, a raft – or the boys might – and I start picking them up, and piling them together, want to make a teepee too.

Fall harvest. With gardens over and chores lighter, now is the time to move freely and far before the confining snow comes. On the way to winter, it's hard not to look at what's around you with a calculating eye.

No reason to go

"There are days my job is hard to take," said our public health officer friend Bill, as he stirred a spoonful of honey into his tea. "Checking water and restaurants – that's all straightforward enough and fine, but there's the odd complaint or eviction that's pretty tough. Take a few years ago, for instance. I was called in about an old man who was living by himself. He didn't have any family. It was the neighbours who complained. Just the usual: the place was run down, a mess, unfit for human habitation in short. I have to back that kind of thing up. He wasn't sick or anything. They said it smelled bad over there, and they didn't like the idea of him living on his own either. No one would know if he died, they said. They wanted him to be put in the old people's home in town." Bill sighed and rubbed his hand over his head.

"You know, I hate that sort of thing. In the end I had to go over there three times, and he didn't make it easy for me, at least not once he found out what I wanted. Damn it, I have to do my job, but I don't think it's right. A man ought to be able to stay on his own land until either he's ready to leave or he dies. That old man wasn't ready.

"Sure, his place was a mess. It wasn't much more than a run-down old shed, but he'd lived there all his life. He didn't get out any more, and he didn't have a phone, but he had it all worked out with the mail carrier to bring a box of groceries once a week and leave it by his mailbox at the end of the drive. He was doing alright, though the neighbours couldn't see it.

"I remember the first time I went over there was a good fall day like this and he was out sitting in an old chair under his apple trees with the apples dropping around him from time to time. Looking over his yard I could see why his neighbours complained. It was a mess – piles of old boards, an old wringer washer, a grindstone, a torn chicken coop with no chickens. There was more stuff lying around outside than there is inside most houses. But seeing the old man walking towards me through that shady light, touching things as he came, I felt like they were his monuments or his family, all pieces out of his past that kept him good company.

"He was good to me that first time. He let me see inside the house, moving around it slowly, always stopping to touch things as if he got something out of them. I'd have to say the place wasn't in good shape. There were old newspapers piled all over the floors, even near the old stove, and the pump in the sink didn't draw any more. I asked him where he got his water and he took me out to the little creek that ran back of the house. The two of us stood there a while, watching the water sparkling over the stones. 'I'm not going, you know,' he said to me. 'I haven't got no reason to go. I've got my land and I can do for myself. Whatever would I want with a place like that?'

"The second time I went out I found him sitting by some bright coloured sumacs out of the wind. 'You'd better go, young man. I'm not leaving and I don't want to see you here again.' He stood up out of his chair trembling, but he wouldn't give in and in the end I had to go.

"The last time I went I didn't see him, but as I got close to the house a shotgun poked out the door. I didn't know what to do so I just walked back to my car and waited, watching the wind blow the last leaves off the old maple by the mailbox. At last he pulled the shotgun out of the door and stood holding the doorframe. He knew it was no use."

The teapot was empty and it was time for Bill to get back to work, but a picture nagged at me all afternoon. I could see a wisp of a man sitting unseen by his window in the old people's home, propped up on his plastic chair just as the nurses had placed him, sitting out his life away from his land just so someone else, any someone, would be there to notice when he died.

The parlour organ

How I missed a piano after I left home. At first, in university, I tried to keep up my playing, but practise rooms were distant and difficult to obtain. Always, when I was at home, I had turned to the piano to work out my ideas and feelings as well as to lose myself in the inventions of my favourite composers. Now I missed fingers and keyboard with an almost physical sense of loss. Sometimes in the first years I secretly resorted to playing an imaginary keyboard much as Trollope's Warden sawed away at his imaginary cello. For a few foolish minutes I could imagine I had recaptured that wonderful feeling of drawing out and shaping the notes again. Later, I sought my lost piano in similar things. My typing became lilting, and I discovered the rhythm of the loom. In weaving I even found a notation similar to the musical staff. I watched the cloth roll from my loom and imagined it was music made visible. Always, I was drawn to pianos I met, but I was forced to know that piano playing now existed only in my imagination.

Then one day Barry and I sat under the elm in front of our pioneer house, watching the yellow leaves swirl about us. It would soon be my birthday, but we weren't thinking about birthdays that year. We had chosen a year away from work, and we weren't regretting it, but we were counting our money in terms of one teabag a day and one beer apiece on a Saturday night.

"Do you hear a noise?" Barry asked, and I lifted my head to listen.

"It sounds like it's just another hay wagon," I said, and stopped. Why would a hay wagon be coming down our lane two months after the farmer had cut and removed all our hay?

"It's Clayton, and he's got Gerald and Gordon with him. That looks almost like furniture standing on the wagon," Barry said. I looked and saw the three sons of our dear neighbours Alva and Sylvia, Clayton, the eldest, driving the tractor, and the twins on the wagon steadying the handsomest parlour organ I had ever seen.

At that point my mind clicked into other time, that time when everything becomes a dream-like haze. In the haze I saw the grins on the faces of the boys. I watched the wagon approach our back door and saw the boys and Barry roll the organ down off the wagon and through our back-kitchen door. Still in a dream I saw them roll the splendid organ through to our sparse livingroom, with its peeling wallpaper and mattress couch. The boys turned to me, but I was speechless.

"I couldn't buy you a piano," Clayton said, "but I knew of this organ. The man up the way had been keeping it in his back-kitchen without heat, which I knew was not good for it. I'd done some work for him and we got along well, so I asked him if he would sell it. And he gave it to me for ten dollars. He wouldn't have sold it to just anyone.

"See, he had ordered it special for his favourite daughter for Christmas, back in the twenties. It came and he hid it away for a surprise, but then the girl took appendicitis and died before he could give it to her. We didn't have the hospital nearby then. So the organ was put away and was never played. I took it home and fixed a few of the reeds, and here it is. It's not a piano, but..."

Somehow I stumbled my disbelieving thanks and the boys left. Barry and I stood admiring the parlour organ as it stood like a queen at the end of the room, with dark, polished wood and crimson plush pedals. There were candlestands and fretwork – so many added touches. At last I walked over and touched the keys hesitantly and then solidly.

"Aren't you going to play it?" Barry asked, and I pulled up a chair and started to pump. The old organ swelled with air and I began sounding it out with chords, my joy mounting as I drew the music from the never-used keys.

Miss Fanny

The first four months after we adopted our half-wild skunk, we doubted she would ever be happy with us. Everyone who knew skunks had warned us that, to become a loving pet, a skunk must be taken before it is weaned and has learned to be defensive. Our cowering, hissing five month old had little reason to want anything to do with humans.

Her mother had been run over the previous summer. In a well-meaning, misguided attempt to make amends, the driver had taken our baby skunk to be descented, a tricky and potentially dangerous operation that must have terrified the wild orphan. As a pet the little one had not worked out. The driver had passed her on to a farm boy who had tamed her somewhat. When summer ended, school and chores had meant the skunk stayed shut in her cage in the barn.

We had always wanted a skunk but we didn't want it to be descented and didn't want to take it from the wild. Yet how could we turn down this challenge? No one else would want a surly, full-grown skunk and the alternative, her release into a strange territory at hibernation time without the protection of scent glands – was unthinkable.

It was unthinkable, at least, in the optimism of the first night when Barry and I and the boys stood back from the cage and watched the skunk drag her heavy-hipped body out of the cage and hustle off behind a large work table. "I didn't know skunks were so small, Mom," whispered Jeremy excitedly. "She's not even as big as the cats."

Unfortunately, during the next two weeks we saw very little more of her as she took up residence behind the table, only appearing to bolt her dish of cat food. (Nothing puts a skunk off its food, we were to learn.)

We quickly came to love the skunk in the same unreasoned way parents love a crying, colicky baby. We gave her a grand name, Miss Fanny Day, on account of her elegant stripes, plumy tail and dainty feet, and promptly shortened the name to 'Fanny' in honour of her best feature.

As much a thief as she was a loner, she hauled off every hank of wool on my lower weaving shelves to feather her nest. I was prepared to scold when I peered in on her, but the sight of the scruffy beast curled up, clinging to a skein of wool as a baby might to a doll, was too much for me, and I withdrew, leaving Fanny with her multicoloured woolly lair.

Barry, who loved her best of all, spent evenings trying to coax her to his hand with bits of cheese. After the first hard bite he took to wearing work gloves, but Fanny soon showed skunk teeth can bite right through heavy leather. When I suggested it was time to give up he protested, "Look at her little black eyes, Peri. She's just full of fear. I've got to make her trust us." Talking to me, he turned too swiftly and, "Hiss, stamp," Fanny the phantom was gone again.

It was a triumph when she grudgingly stood still and let him stroke her back, but she plainly wouldn't accept love. Most worrisome was the frantic way she ran back and forth for hours every night, covering the same spot hundreds of times. It reminded us of animals pacing endlessly in confinement, only Fanny was not locked up. By the end of February we were forced to face the fact that she was desperately unhappy with us.

"Come on, Peri," Barry said as we watched her frenzied dashes one night. "It's never going to get any better. She'll never be happy here. She's a wild animal and she should have stayed that way. We're going to have to let her go and take her chances." I looked at the pitiful animal tracking relentlessly and in my heart I agreed with him. Miss Fanny was unhappy with us, defenceless in the wild. There was no place for her. As soon as the weather warmed up we would release her. I turned sadly away from the pitiful, haggard little animal.

I'm not sure what caused her to change. At the beginning of March wild female skunks would be nearly at the end of their hibernation, so perhaps Fanny's mood responded to the approaching spring outside. At this time we also began to give her vitamin supplements which may have helped. Skunks adjust poorly to any change. Perhaps the shock of being orphaned, descented and shunted through three very different homes had left scars that took a long time to heal. The wonderful thing was that, just as we were despairing, Fanny began to warm to us.

One night as I sat on the rug petting one of our cats I realized that I was not hearing the wretched aimless pattering with which Fan generally filled her nights. I glanced up and saw the skunk squatting in the doorway watching me intently, as if she had forgotten what loving could be like and seeing the cat arch up against my hand brought back memories for her. A few nights later Barry held out her food dish for her and she hustled over to it without stamping once. For the first time she did not freeze when he stroked her and he discovered how supple her skin was, a defence mechanism that helps skunks squirm away from their predators.

Miss Fanny. Once the change came and she let down her defenses against us, she assumed a place in our family very quickly. By Easter she sought out luxuriant petting. So eager was she to make up for lost time that, clumsy as she was, she learned to haul herself up on our couch so she could drape herself over Barry's lap. She developed a passion for popcorn, and her idea of a fine night consisted of being wedged between us on the couch, crunching as many kernels as she could beg or steal. Afterwards she got off the couch with a sinking plop and squatted at our feet to wash her long front digging claws.

As she became more self-assured, Fan found secretive, skunkish games to play, mainly based on thievery. Unwisely, I left a basket of crab apples on the floor, only to look down and notice that half the basket was missing. I watched and in a few minutes an audacious skunk rolled an apple out with her claws, stuffed it between her pointed jaws and trundled off to store it in a corner already piled with booty.

Another night she discovered the fine clatter an empty plastic container could make, and, no longer painfully sensitive to sounds, she spent a gleeful half hour rolling and pouncing with it on the kitchen floor.

At last Fanny had time to notice the animals who shared her surroundings, a kind of notice the three cats, Grog and Bun, the rabbit didn't appreciate. It was past time these animals learned proper respect for skunks, she decided, and, with a majestic indifference to her lack of spray to back up her threats, this smallest of our pets roared around the house striking fear into all. First she sneaked up to the genial and unsuspecting Bun and plunged her needle teeth briskly into the rabbit's forearm. Naturally, there was outrage and alarm, which encouraged

Fan to chivy her all around the kitchen. The cats, quickly learning that skunks can't climb, skirted disdainfully over furniture and windowsills to avoid her attack. The dog to this day has not learned how much of the stamping and headstands routine is a bluff and still rolls his eyes and moans as if to say "If you must have this hateful thing in the house, surely you could keep her under some order."

Now, two years after we brought the trembling, hostile orphan home, I watch Miss Fanny sniffing her way around her accustomed routes, a lurching wonder of a skunk, and I marvel again at the love and friendship we have thrashed out between us.

Leaves for Red Lake

Fall was a disappointment to me the year I lived in northwestern Ontario. The first blow came when I missed hearing the cries of wild geese flying overhead. People told me that the flyway passed only sixty miles away, but we had no car and no hope of going to the geese who didn't come to us. For the first time, I saw snow before Thanksgiving, and the cold was not relieved by an Indian summer. As I was to find out, things were only going to get colder and bleaker over the long months until a late spring arrived the following May.

Autumn came for one brief week. The aspens and birches, the only deciduous trees that had returned to the fire-wasted land, turned a brilliant yellow. The trembling leaves sparkled in the least wind, contrasting with the black-green evergreens behind them. But, as I wrote to our friend Clayton back home, it was a landscape without one touch of red. I was glad to have experienced the fleeting northern autumn, but how I missed the maples.

At the end of the week a cold wind raged all night and I awoke to find the trees bare with only a scattering of gold on the ground. From then on the cold numbed my fingers as I hung Morgan's diapers on the line. Often ravens beat the sky over my head with creaking wings of wood. By November it was already dark at three-thirty when the buses pulled away from the school down in the plain where the poplars grew. One day I walked down the big hill into town to collect the mail, with Morgan, then a baby, on my back. Morgan, jouncing and singing to himself, was the only brightness in an austere landscape. I tramped over the frozen mud to the post office and found a card advising me of a package too big for the box. It could be picked up during office hours the next day. Mail of any kind was rare that year, so I willingly repeated my trip the next day, pulling a poncho over Morgan in his carrier to protect him from the drizzle. At the office, the clerk handed over a large but curiously light parcel. So light was the box that I found myself suspicious as I carted it home up the big hill. I had noticed the return address was Clayton's and he and his family were notorious practical jokers. Perhaps I was carrying home only a box of air. Still, I was homesick enough on that cold, damp day that the thought of any package from friends and home warmed me.

Once I had unbundled Morgan and released him to crawl around the floor, I opened my package. There was no note, but then there didn't need to be. The contents spoke for themselves. Inside the box, lovingly pressed and arranged, were the leaves of an eastern Ontario autumn forest. Maple leaves of all sizes and hues, claret ash leaves, rosy ones from oaks and tobacco-brown beech leaves all lay within the box. I could have laughed out loud for pleasure at the rightness of the gift or cried too, if I'd dared to start. But Morgan was pulling himself up curiously on the bedspread, demanding to see the contents too. I sat him on the bed and spilled the calico leaves over him. I watched the slow, spinning fall that I had missed that year. Both of us picked them up and traced the points of the maples and oaks and fingered the ribs of the beeches. "Leaf," I said to Morgan, delightedly. "oh, leaf." Gently we rumpled them and I tried to get the leaf-kicking feeling that had passed me by. I buried my nose in the pile and smelled their ripe, sweet scent. While we played, I had an idea that came because I wanted to keep the leaves with me and relieve the sterility of our rented bungalow. I got a needle, threaded the leaves onto varying lengths of black thread and hung the streamers of leaves in a group over the bed.

All winter the leaf mobile hung in the bedroom, with the gay leaves swaying and rustling to the slightest current. Morgan laughed and kicked when he lay under it and I slipped in often each day to lift my spirits, watching the swirl of the leaf dance.

A patch of blue sky is enough

It was the start of our second hour in a dreary waiting room. I glanced impatiently out a window that revealed only a brick wall and a space of empty blue sky. "How ugly it is here," I said impatiently to my artist father. "There is simply nothing for the eye to rest on."

"No," he corrected me, "as long as you have sky to look at you're all right. Think of prisoners who keep sane in solitary confinement when all they have is a tiny window on the sky. Think of sailors alone on the vast ocean, studying the sky with the keenest interest because their lives depend on what they see, the wheeling of clouds and stars."

"I don't know how long I could be content not having trees and hills to look at," I objected.

"But that's just it," he said eagerly. "Most people never even look up. They spend their lives always looking down at their feet. You could ask them if the sky was clear or cloudy and they wouldn't know."

With so many things worth seeing, I don't confine myself to the sky often, but I began to think back to a week I had spent in bed with only the changes in the sky at my window to watch. By the time I could get up, I had felt more intimate with the passing clouds than with the hectic goings-on of my family on the floor below.

As I thought about what my father had said I decided I would find it hard to be content with a sky in a dry climate that reflected only the passing of night and day. It was the play of a variable climate that made it compelling for me. I remembered looking up to see the air tumbling with snow. I thought of the queer, dangerous light that preceded a tornado.

Actually, as I went back over notable skies, I realized that in our climate the sky was rarely the same two days in a year. I saw that there was much more scope for observation than I had ever imagined. Why does everything look so different when the sun is going down from what it does when it is coming up, I mused. There must be more involved than the relocation of the sun to the west. If all one had to watch was sky, how many variations and relationships would appear?

If I could choose my patch I'd want one close to where land and sky meet rather than at the dome, even although I would miss the swift-flying clouds of the upper air. It is the washes of colour along the sky's border that I find most beautiful. I'd want my piece of sky to include the occasional sunrise streaked with crimson from its most transparent to its most intense range.

I thought back to what my father had said about sailors and their reliance on sky for signs of weather and navigation. A large part of our need for sky is orientation of various kinds, I decided. Being able to see a band of streaky cloud puts things into place. "Oh, I remember another day with clouds like that," you'll say. "That was the day Jim left home." Of course the sky contains the sun's path and the stars' movements too, and following their constancy gives point to our lives, helps us navigate past the less predictable events of the day. The sky's aspect helps us steady our position with weather as well. Although anyone who has experienced a flash flood or a relentless drought knows we cannot control weather, the predictions we can make studying the sky give us a sense of control over our place with it. The black cloud moving in swiftly warns me to urge my boys into the house before the lightning reaches us. The steel of a winter sky makes me put out fresh seed for the birds before the coming snow.

A gull sailed past the waiting room window and I thought that it was true: a patch of sky is all you really need. From azure to rose to ash, the sky had changed as we sat in the waiting room. "Mrs. McQuay," the nurse beckoned, and I turned away from our sky and walked into the office.

Country fire

The last crimson leaves of the Virginia creeper vine that climbed around the window were twisting restlessly in a fitful wind. It was a dark afternoon in November ten years ago. Three-months-old Jeremy was sick and I had spent the early afternoon rocking him and looking dreamily over the drab fields. Outside the window the wind rose and fell, tugging at the sodden leaves lying under the lilac bushes.

I shifted my baby to my other shoulder and looked up to see two strangers in suits peering in the half-window of the door. So few people travelled our back road in November that I hesitated to go to them until they started pounding on the door and pointing down the road. "Didn't you see?" exclaimed the smaller man. "Who lives in the house down the road from you? There's smoke coming out all over the place. We tried to get in but it's locked. You'll have to call the fire department."

The men rushed off down the road again and I dialed the number for the local fire fighters, trying unsuccessfully to believe that something urgent could be happening on such a hazy day. Only after I had made my call did I walk to the other side of the house to look over the fields towards the McNamee's beautiful brick farmhouse. Then began an afternoon that gave me a whole new feeling for country living, both for the ungrudging generosity of neighbours and for the relentless power of fire.

It was true. As if it were a painting of a house on fire I saw the house with crazy curls of smoke hiding the warm red of the old bricks. If only I had been on this side of the house I would have seen the smoke sooner. As I watched, a puff of wind licked the smoke at the back into a flame. I opened the door and listened; in the distance was a scene out of a nightmare, and, as in a nightmare, sound was muffled.

As a woman alone with a small baby, I felt helpless. I could not leave my house. The phone call, made too late, was the only help I could give. Back and forth, back and forth I walked before the window, watching the smoke gathering around the distant house.

If only someone would come quickly. And then I saw something I'll never forget, tangible proof that caring lives on in the country. Only ten minutes after the men left my door the first car raced down the road. Men in work clothes jumped out, slammed their doors and raced towards the burning house, followed quickly by a stream of cars and trucks until the line stretched back over the hill and out of sight. Even before the volunteers could get to the fire station the party-line phones and rising smoke had done their job.

As I watched the treacherous path of the fire and saw how the best efforts of the volunteers and the large crowd of men were powerless to slow it, I learned that a fire can have an uncontrollable life of its own. Unless it is caught early, a country fire is likely to be hopeless. At best the outbuildings will be saved.

Some time after the first rush of cars, Diane and Michael returned from Christmas shopping to find their home past saving and joined in the sorry job of dragging out what precious belongings they could. The darkness was coming in quickly but the cruel light of the flames illuminated fragments around the house. A piano appeared on the lawn. A little boy stood back clutching a large book. Bent over, I saw a woman clinging to another woman.

After nightfall the fire subsided and slowly the long column of trucks and cars left. The sudden November fire extinguished forever the homelight that had shone from the old brick house for so many years, but I was aware of another kind of warmth, one that held country people together. Long into the night the rural phone kept ringing two long rings to our neighbours' parents down the road with messages of concern and help.

Land longing

Looking for land: it's a lot like looking to be in love. The search is poignant and often unreasonable. "It's got to be perfect," a friend confided, speaking of the place she was looking for. "We want it to have a brook, a barn in good repair, a maple bush, and it must be close to town.

Every spring we read the real estate ads, pare them down to credibility and venture out with topographical maps unfurled and high hopes. It's a quest, the dream of a place of our own, and like all such searches, it holds moments of high expectation and intense enjoyment. For the past eighteen years we've looked, and although we haven't found our place, we have found a hidden lake after a mile-long trip through small woods, a lane full of morels, fields where marsh hawks skim the grass and a shallows from which three herons rose.

As in seeing a person through the bloom of love, the hundreds of acres we've searched have taken on a shiny, heightened reality in our memories. We've learned to read the landscape both for our own needs and for our hopes for its own wellbeing. How would it be, we let ourselves ask, to travel this curving lane each day? We look at the colour and depth of soil and at the plants it sends up. Here is where we could put our garden. Are there beeches and pines, oaks and maples, birches and hemlocks in the woods, I ask? I ask, much as I once asked Barry if he liked Jane Austen, Hopkins and Jean Giono. We look at the curves of the property and discuss earnestly the quality of its water. I try to keep my eyes on the shelter value of the spruces behind the home site and away from the water lilies on the distant pond.

But a promised land doesn't come easily, and when August arrives without success, I begin to remind myself that land cannot truly be bought anyway. It owns itself. All we can do is care for it. As it is with the best love that lives long after fascination, the owner of land supports and strengthens it and leaves his mark on it only lightly. To do all this I need not own the land; I can as easily care for others'.

Yet the longing will not go away. We visit property that still has the original deed and has been handed down through five generations. At the back of a field we find an old foundation, a briar rose, rhubarb and asparagus ferns. When you buy land you do more: you buy the right to a kinship with the other owners. In reality, this place costs far more than we can afford, but for a foolish moment I think, "If I went to the owners and told them we would share their love for it, would prize their roots, take strength from them and care for this place for the rest of our lives..."

In late fall we pack it in for another year and turn away from the advertised "Shangri-las" and "Woodsman's Specials". We're too late. It's too late. My eyes are tight as we drive home. I don't look back at the hill swooping up to the sky or the nightmarish slash of brush that is all that remains of a woods where we used to hear mourning doves and watch the trees flower each spring.

I once had a friend who set his hopes on some land, saved for it and coaxed the owner to sell. Then it was his. The papers were in progress and one day he drove out to look it over with the fresh eyes of ownership, only to find that the maples bigger than arm spans were gone. "I never said anything about the wood going with the place," said the former owner.

Buying land, like finding love, can be treacherous, I remind myself. Perhaps we'll never find this land of our own. As the trees fall and the prices rise, I see it receding more every year. Dreams often don't come true. But sometimes, living in their illumination is enough.

Sombre

For once the woods was uninviting, dark and wet. As I entered its threshold by an overgrown path, wiry branches stung my face and a gust of wind brought a flurry of raindrops through the bare trees down upon my head.

Usually I like to wander freely through the woods, but on such an unpleasant day I was out only to clear my head, so I decided to take a faster route and follow Jake's old lane. Once Indian Jake had made the lane as a carriageway through the woods to the secluded cabin where he made chairs for a living. In places saplings had grown up now, obscuring the way, but often two slight, even ruts could still be seen curving around rocks and large trees. At one place the sides of the ascent of a hill were buttressed with carefully placed, moss-grown stones. I liked to follow the trail, remembering the man whose sympathy with this woods had more than likely surpassed my own.

Walking the trail as briskly as I could, I tried not to notice all the evidence around me that, although winter and its snow had not yet arrived, fall was over. Water from many rains was lying everywhere, and I paused to peer into one of the black pools. Through its magnifying clarity I could see the once-crisp leaves lying on the bottom. From all the leaves in the pools and on the forest floor the stain was fading fast. Even the crisp oak and beech leaves that still held fast to their branches had lost some of their ochre colouring.

On such a late fall rainy day the woods is more subdued, I thought, than at almost any other time of the year. My feet passed almost soundlessly over the dead, wet leaves and I heard only the odd, imperfect fragment of a bird call through the chill, still-moving air. Only in smell did the woods seem rich. There was a pervasive, dank fragrance of decaying leaves and rich, rotting logs.

At some distance I heard a grouse drumming with untimely vigour. As always, it sounded to me like the pulse of the woods, and, hearing that life on such an unlikely day, I stepped off the path into a clearing, trying to guess where the grouse might be. The throbbing call ended as abruptly as it had begun, and I saw that I was in what at first appeared to be a rocky, barren clearing. As I stood hoping that the drumming would be repeated, however, I realized that the rocks were not really barren at all because of the profusion of deep mosses and hoary lichens that covered them. Here at least was something that relished the steady rains. I had never seen such a lovely dappling of bright and deep green mosses and among the lichens I bent to admire the scarlet cups of the British Soldiers species.

I bent over, but then I recoiled. Stretched across the moss was a stark trail of chalky bones, perfectly cleared of flesh. The skeleton was scattered like the random phrases of an unfinished poem. At first I was repelled by its bleakness in the gloom of the woods, but as I studied its parts, trying to decide what creature had died, I began to appreciate their exquisite symmetry, the winged coil of the spine, the delicate, finely shaped teeth. Likely it had been prey for the foxes who haunted Jake's trail and the nearby glades. Yes, there were fox scats on a number of the rocks. Who knew who else had taken part in the feast as well? Deep in the clefts of the rocks I saw the casings of insects, now moved on to other states and sizes, and yet all who had dined last summer on the dead animal would some day be as this slight linkage of bare bones. I fingered a flanged joint, gently measuring the green, creeping moss that had adhered to its base, beginning its decay.

Decay. Crouched over the bones, reflecting on mortality, I heard the approach of a small troop of nuthatches, brash and full of life. I listened to their feathery flight and watched them rap their way up the pines at the edge of the clearing, digging insects out from under the bark. Their vitality illuminated the clearing, and when they moved on, as abruptly as they had appeared, I looked around, surprised at the colour I had missed before. The pioneers called the darker shades "sad colours", but even these were welcome before the black and white of winter. There was the hectic green of frost-bitten strawberry leaves and wild grasses, and over rocky hummocks trailed canes of mahogany raspberry leaves. Wintergreen and partridgeberry, fed by the rains, were dense and deeply green, plentifully spotted with red berries. In winter these would provide food for the creatures that could dig deeply enough through the snow to find them, and in the spring, before the grasses began to grow, these mosses, leaves and berries would give survivors a good start after the long, taxing winter. At last I could accept that even here in the heart of the forest, on one of the darkest days of the year, there was still colour and the challenge of life's mutability, if I became still enough to see deeply. Even the quickening rain couldn't chill me now.

The friendly fox

All it takes is a rusty oak leaf blowing across the snow under the feeder for me to think I see the fox again. In these years at the peak of the rabies cycle, foxes have a tainted character. Ask anyone around here and he'll give you a story of a vicious attack by a rabid fox. Some of the stories likely are true. Rabies must be respected, but when I think of foxes, I don't think of dangerous, dying animals, I think of the fox, our fox, I call her, if friendship counts for anything.

Barry saw her first two autumns ago, the fox who moved in a shadow ballet around our lives. She entered the scene with a leap of bravado while he was raking leaves, or, as he tells it, "I felt as if something was staring at me and when I turned around a fox rushed at me. I grabbed onto the rake; I was sure she was rabid, but at the last she skidded to a stop and went racing off, sending my leaves flying. She stayed around me for about a half hour, prancing and capering, tail high in the breeze. When at last she started to go off into the bushes, something of her foolishness got into me and I quacked at her like a duck. She whirled around and started all over again, frisking and chasing her tail. I never before saw a fox who wanted anything to do with me."

Then came a November night with a bright moon and an unreasonably warm wind. I put the dog out on his chain and returned to finish my book. It was a pleasant night for Grog to be out and I became engrossed in what I was reading. In short, it was nearly an hour before I went back out to retrieve Grog, and I found his collar was torn in two and he was gone. As I stared at the collar, I heard his feet pounding around the field and short, excited barks, some of which were undoglike. Near and distant the barks came, entirely indifferent to my calling and at last I watched in disbelief as Grog and a fox ran side by side over the rocks in the moonlight.

It was not until morning that Grog limped wearily home, Grog who had wrenched off his collar, called by something so wild there was no resisting. Now Grog, who is neutered, slunk up on the porch, appearing, to my eyes at least, embarrassed, and the fox, who apparently had sought him for a mate, did not appear to us again until snow was on the ground.

Many times that winter we saw her. Often I heard the jays scolding and looked out to see her slink to the feeder and snap at crusts. Now her kittenish play of the fall was gone. Winter was deadly serious for the fox, and I looked out on her obvious hunger with pity. More than cold had taken its toll on her too. A large flap of skin hung loose from the side of her muzzle, hampering her feeding. After she had seized her crusts, she looked up at me, standing close by in the open doorway, with a speaking glance I will not forget, and then flitted off in her shadowy way across the hard snow.

Some nights, if we put on the porch light and looked out we saw her sitting before our door asking for what: food, Grog's company, affection? We'll never know, but we came to believe that the oak-leaf coloured fox must have been somebody's discard, a pet no longer wanted who was released into the park. It was true, she did survive in dog-like fashion, but for her there was something wilderness could not give.

In the end I am left with the picture of her that my son Morgan gave me. It was the last time any of us saw her. "I was picking wild strawberries over near the pines and there she was, only an arm's length away, eating big mouthfuls of berries, with the hot sun shining on her red fur."

We never saw her again and we'll never know whether she died naturally or whether she met a bullet from a countryman understandably afraid of such unnatural friendliness in a wild animal. "She was beautiful, Mom, and she wasn't afraid," Morgan said.

A barn lament

The first and only barn I ever lived with is gone, I see. When I drove by last fall all that remained of it was a scaffolding standing dripping in the cold rain. I stopped to visit a former neighbour and he told me it went for barnboard. An entrepreneur had toured the back roads and the owner had not found it worth his while to turn him down. He (the entrepreneur) must have done quite well for himself, the neighbour guessed, because barns all around that way torn down now. He supposed all that board went to decorate restaurants in Ottawa. It was a shame, my neighbour agreed, but he guessed there wasn't much use for barns anymore with everyone quitting farming.

I drove on along familiar roads that wet November day and saw that my neighbour was right. The exposed bones of former barns confronted me repeatedly and I returned home saddened by the loss of those landmarks and vowing not to drive that way again. But I couldn't resist going back. This time I found that even the hand-hewn timber of the frames had gone, cut down and consumed, I supposed, as a result of the ever-increasing demand for firewood.

My barn and its like are vanishing from the landscape, so I'm glad I still have a collection of ghostly barns, larger than life as things seen in memory tend to be. The first barn I remember is the one where I took shelter from the high afterwinds of Hurricane Hazel. I had been cooped up in a tiny summer cottage by the rain until I (and my parents too, I imagine) could no longer stand it and I went to try out the swing I'd been told was in the hayloft. I began to imagine forts and castles lurking in the shadows of the piled-up bales. I sniffed the summer fragrance of the hay and felt the barn grow taut and give like a sail before a variable wind. Somewhere overhead I could hear the broody cooing and flapping of pigeons.

Hanging on long, hand-thick ropes from far over my head was a swing. I went over to it and pumped my way back and forth in broad arcs over the hay. This was no relation to a tame playground swing. Gaining in courage I stood up on the swing and let myself fly through the air on the upstrokes, reaching almost to the pigeons, then swooping giddily down. Outside was a dangerous storm but within I was both safe and free. Ever since, when I've needed a refuge I've thought of the barn tossing off the hurricane. I've remembered the sounds and the scents, the soundness and the fractured light through the chinks.

Long afterwards Barry and I and Morgan rented a farmhouse that had a fine big barn on its adjacent property and we came to know it in all its seasons. Morgan and I watched its doors open to accept load after load of hay in summer until the bales made steppingstones for him that led to the tiny ventilation window at the peak of the roof. "You can see all over the world from here, Mom," said my three-year-old son. He and our then young and stealthy dog Grog had secrets in all the crannies of the barn. When friends came for the weekend it was the two of them who showed the visitors where to find the pigeons' nests and where the best hiding spots were for hide-and-seek. Even our city friends, we found, gravitated to the barn.

In winter Barry and I slipped in at the bottom entrance, thankful for the cattle's steamy warmth as we looked for the new calf our farm neighbour who rented the barn had invited us to see.

When I was troubled, it was the barn I sought out. I wedged myself in among the bales where a dusty shaft of sunlight could reach me and absorbed the peace until I felt ready to go back to the house again.

Early in the morning I looked out across the field to the barn looming in the mist and last thing at night I looked over at it, ashen in the moonlight. When we left that place, the last thing I saw was the barn, standing like a grey mother, knee-deep in snow.

It's taken me a long time to face thinking about what was lost when that barn was torn down. When I look across spreading fields to a great galleon of a wooden barn, I see a living organism. The web of life that a working barn sustains, from fungus to hay, from insect to spider to swallow, from grain to mouse to barn owl, is amazing in its diversity. A barn commands respect because it is a vibrant house of life. Barns are compelling, too, because, since biblical days and beyond, they have been symbols of prosperity, storehouses, speaking of something left over for a bad time. Once a farmer had a barn safely raised he had the promise of security, food and shelter wrapped in one structure. Then security was tied up with an essential feeling of being able and obliged to provide for oneself. Food, as the storehouse barn proclaimed, came first. Now we have new symbols of security. If you wish to appear prosperous, you do not fill a fine barn, you drive an expensive car manufactured by someone you'll never know. Now barns not only stand empty, but also are disappearing from our way of life.

Of course, they were built during different economic times. Who now could afford to erect a building as generous as a barn? What they call a barn where I live now, is a new, poor, spindly thing, built partly of two-by-four's. But it cost more to build by far than did the solid shelters of earlier days.

Barns may have been symbols of independence but they required a communal effort to raise them. In those days no one could afford not to care about neighbours. Sometimes I turn to the chapter "Food For a Barn Raising" in my Mennonite cookbook and read of seventy-five pies and other delights. For a few minutes I can see the gaiety, the resourcefulness and the hard work, followed by the very tangible rewards of a new barn. Barn raising – the very words have sound of cheer to them, like flags snapping in a breeze on a sunlit day. But the barns are going now. They're no longer needed, I'm told. And I close my cookbook and put it away.

I can still recall vividly the interior of that barn I lost. I used to run my hands over the huge, square-cut timbers, tasting the solid smoothness and examining the marks of cleavage where the wood had been shaped with hand tools. When I think of intrinsic beauty I think of the joinery of a barn. All of the frame is fitted together without a single nail; the joints are simple but handsome as right-fitting things are. Moreover, having laboured a few evenings over mortises and tenons, I can appreciate the skill it must have taken to fashion joints that would support so large and heavy a structure. This craftsmanship was a necessary part of every countryman's heritage, pointing him towards independence.

In one more way the massive beams reflected the past and that was in their size. Whoever cut and burned the skeleton of that barn destroyed the last evidence that once there had been trees large enough to take the barn's stresses. Once there had been forests that could have supported the temperate farmer in his wants forever. Now they were gone as was the timber they had provided. Once too, for that matter, there had been fields not always wisely husbanded. Now the fields no longer could feed their owners and the barns, no longer of use, were cut down.

I still know where I can find a good barn if I need one in time of trouble or joy, but I find myself wondering how my children will manage.

A pine's death

On a black night at end of fall and the beginning of winter the pine fell. A high wind stormed through its flailing branches, its roots groaned and there was a clap like thunder. The earth shivered as it received the tree and then was still.

The pine had been in trouble for some time. Growing in poor, shallow soil, its roots had been assaulted by several summers of drought in which they had dwindled. Then they had rotted during a summer of heavy rain that flooded their inadequate system. Then there followed a fall of high winds that tore at the tree, heaving what roots it had left until great cracks appeared in the soil at its base. Into these cracks water seeped and lingered to further work on the dying roots. At night the squirrels nesting in a neighbouring oak could hear the ooze and suck as the pine made its last efforts to cling to the forest soil.

As the death of the roots heralded the end of the failing tree, other assailants seized the chance to feed on its dying. All trees are hosts to many forms of plants and animals that feed on them, but in health they can support this life without suffering themselves. But because the roots could no longer nourish the pine, its bark had become loose. Carpenter ants and beetles began to tunnel up into the wood, opening it to other attackers. Fungi grasped the openings and plunged long, microscopic roots deep into the tree, feeding on it and breaking into it still further. The woodpeckers whose search for insects would cleanse a sound tree, tore at the loose bark and opened the tree still further to decay. The stage was set for its decomposition.

When the winds tore the pine out by the roots and toppled it, in a sense it died, but in a more significant way it had moved on to another, but equally fruitful state. The morning after the pine collapsed, the stubs of its roots could be seen clawing the air. The soil that clung to them was sandy pale and told the story of the tree's failure plainly. Wedged in the claw-like roots were some of the rocks that had thwarted the roots' efforts to strike deep. Now, in its death, the tree would begin its work of improving the soil that had been unable to sustain it.

The moisture that had been the dying tree's enemy now worked with it. The cavity where once the roots had grown now became a container for the late fall rain that followed the wind storm. This hollow would work as a reservoir to filter the water slowly into the soil. During the next few years emerald mosses would grow thickly over the arm-like branches and the trunk, eating into the bark and rooting into the log.

Now that the pine lay in close contact with the earth and no longer was readily cleansed by the air, bacteria, unseen but voracious feeders, took a free hand in the disintegration of the tree. At the same time a procession of larger predators and prey began to dine off the tree. Insects bored into the bark to lay eggs which hatched into grubs which in turn drilled their way out again through wider holes. Earthworms fed off the decayed flesh of the tree, adding their goodness to it by way of their castings. All the time the decomposing matter was being stirred and altered by these various feasters at the death.

As the diners came so did their predators. A host of active shrews sifted through the new earth seeking out the insects and worms. The rotting tree, although no longer alive itself, was quick with all the life it supported. Larger creatures came too. Skunks, raccoons and bears ripped at the wood with their long digging claws, and, in their search, laid it open to still more decay.

Over the next fifty to one hundred years the decaying tree would go on feeding the forest community, and, by doing so, would replenish one of the most precious resources we have, living soil. Because of the fallen pine, the next tree seedlings to drive down roots would face a better chance of life, for, without death and decay there would be no life.

Fear in the woods

"Don't you worry going about alone like that? What if you broke an ankle and nobody found you for hours?" a friend asked once. I could only answer that I'd be more worried if I *didn't* go into the woods.

But I always face an edge with my first steps within a forest. It's an edge that is a cross between "the call of the wild" and "If you go down in the woods today, you're sure of a big surprise." It's expectancy coupled with a slight awareness of danger that sharpens my senses and shakes me awake. I am more careful where and how I walk when I go alone, and if conditions are bad I leave a note saying where I plan to go. But that edge says it all. Without the woods I'd be nothing. Fear no longer seems like a good reason to avoid something. If I go with it, not recklessly but lightly, the fear helps me slip into another gear.

I'll never be able to smell what my dog does when he stands on the rocks, ears blowing and nose to the wind, but as I lope down into a valley, the tea-leaf smell of dead leaves is all about me. Beautiful. At the depth of the valley another scent intrudes, though, the cloying smell of decay and fear is with me again. The leaves are wet and muffled, and I stand in a cleft between two rocky walls, here for the taking. Any predator can stalk me unheard. This is not my woods. I don't know the safe places. My head snaps around. I've heard nothing; it is only the smell that troubles me. Death is in the air. It may stand poised above that tumble-down rock slide or slink behind the beeches ahead of me.

I've never seen a buck in rut, but I've heard they can become crazed. Their season should be over and yet... Deer lunge away from me in winter, radiant with fear. But now, in autumn, could it be that I am at risk? Still there is the smell. I begin to canvass the trees, thinking in terms of flight upwards if not onwards. As my search widens I hear the slow music of water dripping over the rocks. High on the beeches I notice old scars, ripped there, I imagine, by the claws of a bear. Bear. Even the woodsmen around here say "bear" in a different tone. My heart thuds. Climb? No. Anything I could climb he could climb better. Run? No, oh, no. His sinewy strides would outrun me any day. Out of the corners of my eyes (even my eyes are motionless now) I search for black fur, or perhaps a cloud of breath-steam.

Gradually the woods that has been racing around me stills. Nothing has challenged me. I put out a foot and then the other and I reach up to touch the scars on the beech. It is hibernation time now, when bears are satiated, I tell myself, and the scars are well-healed, made some other year.

The blanched leaves still hanging from the tree stand out like warnings, but I know now I must make my move. I walk past the beech and follow the valley out to a beaver pond. I am walking more easily now, but still I notice that I hug the shoulder of granite that contains the pond. My feet are practising their steps, gauging the slipperiness of wet lichen on rock and sounding each landing. As my stride shifts to a swing I realize I have a sharper sense of my place in the woods now. I am as taut and limber as a bow-string. I sense bears in the woods, weigh their threat and move on, glorying in the mosses beneath my feet. Wild bears, fearing man, rarely show themselves, I know. We in the woods share fear. By grace of my fear, I am closer to predators and prey.

Winter

Making peace with winter

On a bleak day in early December I stand watching the stone-coloured water crackle against the rind of ice on the shoreline of our lake. Overhead I hear the sound of whistling wingbeats and look up to watch one of the final migrations of the year. Even the goldeneyes, the last ducks to linger with us, are fleeing now, but I – and I scuff glumly at the frozen sand – must stay on to face our long cold winter.

The whistlers soon pass and I am left to try to make my peace with the approaching season. This feeling of resentment is new to me, although many older friends have smiled and told me how inevitable it is. "You're just getting older like the rest of us, that's all," they say. Other years the measuring of the seasons and their progress has seemed fair to me. I've looked at winter with a proper sense of appreciation. If my own spirits ever failed in recent years, they were lifted by the enthusiasm of two boys who cannot get enough of snow.

Winter. More than ever before I have resisted coming to grips with its approach. Earlier I sought out the last flowers that echo summer, here one pink clover blossom, further down the road one last blue flower on a faded stalk of viper's bugloss – I even found a raspberry bush snug in the cleft of a rock that still yields a scanty harvest of berries. But on this cheerless day it's hard to deny winter, and I have made a final trip to the shore to say goodbye to the living water.

I pick up a stone and pitch it at the shoreline ice, where, disconcertingly, instead of breaking through, it skates along the surface before slithering over the edge into water. The lake won't be water much longer. The first flakes of the snow that has been heavy in the air all afternoon sting my cheeks. Snow. I might as well say goodbye to the deepest reaches of the woods while I'm at it, I grumble. Very soon now, getting around will be restricted to skis (not very satisfactory in dense rocky woods) and snowshoes, clumsy and tiring.

Two nuthatches alight on a beech tree and begin to scour its surface. Now the migrants are gone all that will be left until March are the common winter birds, I think, and then stop short, shamed by the ingratitude of such a thought. How could anyone feel less than rich watching such spirit? The two move over the tree. As always, I'm fascinated by the way they keep in touch with each other as if they were joined by an unseen bond, until they move farther into the woods where the sound of their chatter relieves the coldness of the day.

My softer feeling for the birds of winter begins to extend itself. As I look out over the lake my mood breaks. I can see that the ice I had resented was deliciously lacy, a rare pattern that I should have been enjoying before the snow hides it. For that matter, the quickening snow against the dark pines is beautiful too.

Winter for me, as for the birds, the lake and the woods is a testing time. I look at the wind-swept curves of the pine. Only those who accept the season's limits will come out enriched by the experience. I will keep coming out of doors until winter becomes a normal state to me, but now I look forward to the warmth of my home. On the counter somewhere there is a new bread recipe that has lain unused all summer while I was out wandering. It would be good to fill the house with its fragrance. On the stair landing waits a whole shelf of new books hoarded away for winter, and I know exactly on which bed I can find three warm and loving cats who have the good sense to adjust to the changing seasons, and would be glad of company.

I turn away from the lake and trudge up the big hill towards home with faster steps, but as I go I look with lightness at the swirling snow that is surrounding me.

Chickadees

Framed by dark pines, a picture stays with me, a picture of a small boy with a long, red touque standing by a bird feeder with his outstretched hand piled with seeds. Far over his head a flock of chickadees darts. Around him big snowflakes fall silently, continuously, as if the scene were set in one of those snowstorm paper-weights that children prize. I can see the boy standing patiently in the falling snow until one uncommonly brash chickadee dips down, seizes a seed and is gone, leaving the boy lit with joy.

Thinking of the boy at the feeder reminds me of the first time I stood by the feeder enjoying the feathery flight of the chickadees all around me and the delight I felt when one touched my bare hand with his claws and seized a seed. Although the bird was small, in spite of feathers fluffed against the cold, the amount of life radiating from his drab grey and white body was striking. With their cheer and individuality, chickadees take a very special place in our winter.

Understandably, the chickadees at the sheltered area of the well feeder where Jeremy stands to hand-feed them are generally more confiding than those at our house feeder, which is situated in the open. What surprises me is that the boldest chickadee we have encountered was one of the house feeder birds.

On a warm day near spring I left the front door propped open while I brought in loads of groceries. When I finished, I heard a fluttery sound in the living room and saw a chickadee flying close to the ceiling. Naturally I was worried. The poor bird must be terrified finding itself confined in a strange place. What would I do if one of the cats, who were indignantly housebound for the duration of bird feeding, chose to come downstairs?

I reopened the front door and began the maddening task of batting my arms delicately to steer out a bird who showed neither distress nor interest in leaving. I had the impression that, contrary to my expectations, it was delighted with its new situation. Its flight was leisurely rather than panicky, and it chirped at me in a gentle way that was quite different from the usual aggressive sound of chickadees in winter. It seemed that, having discovered warmth and houseplants, the bird found the house preferable to the snowy scene outside. I became more convinced of this than ever when the same afternoon a chickadee, surely the same one, startled the boys by pushing past them into the house. This time Barry escorted it to the door tactfully but firmly with the broom and we saw it no more.

Seeing chickadees' good-hearted response to the very real hardship of their winter is inspiring. Their need for food is so demanding that their average life span is only a year and a half. In winter they face a strenuous search for the large amount of food they need to warm their tiny bodies. Yet, for all their need for food is urgent, they move among each other with cheer and with a respect for their pecking order most unlike the evening grosbeaks who squabble so badly that I am amazed that any of them ever get to eat.

Unfortunately, chickadee respect does not extend to Barry who fills their feeders. They only need to glimpse his dark winter coat as he unloads the seed buckets from the truck to set up a cacophony of scolding. Even when he is walking in the woods without seed the birds follow Barry to pester him.

In spite or because of this determined spirit, I keep returning to enjoy the picture of the little bird perched fearlessly in Jeremy's hand. When at last I hear the first poignant "phoebe" of their spring song, I feel it the more for having lived through winter in their company.

An artist's Christmas cards

The year before he died, my artist father collected and mounted the Christmas cards he had designed and printed during a span of more than thirty years. In doing so he gathered and pinned down in a box an artist's life with all its shifts and fluctuations.

As I grew up, each year's new card was central to our Christmas celebration. For days my father pinned up sketches, consulted my mother and reworked angles on tracing paper. My sister and I had to tread lightly and never found it safe even to mention the card's existence. Then one evening a lino block and gouges appeared on his desk. Now, more than ever, we went warily when we played. One false nick and the block would be ruined. One letter that was not correctly reversed and there would be misery and recriminations. If he left his desk, we studied the block surreptitiously, but could make little of the right-to-left lettering and the scratches and hollows.

At last the effort would be over and my sister and I would

become most welcome as printer's assistants. Donning sweaters and jackets, we went down to the cold cellar to work the press while my father mixed the gloriously sticky ink and rolled it onto the block. With the peeling of the first copy a new card came to life for us all and another Christmas became lastingly fixed in a print.

Now I keep the box of cards where I can enjoy them often. First I look at the early cards. There's a woodcut of the house where I grew up, flooded with light on a snowy evening. Next to it is a picture of a tiny girl on a swing with feet tilted skyward, and then there is a card with two girls looking at the stars through an ivy-wreathed window. A few of the cards are my mother's, spirited and graceful, and her inspiration is in all of them.

As I pass on through the cards, I see my father's other world as he travelled by train to and from Toronto and walked the streets each noon hour, sketching endlessly. There is a wheelbarrow bulging with trainman's lamps and a CNR train with steam blowing into the stars. I see a sampling of the Toronto he relished – the old Arcade, Loretto Abbey before it was torn down, a huddle of Christmas spruces at Kensington Market and a commemoration of a post office, designed to appear like a cancelled postage stamp.

When the two little girls at the vine-circled window grew up, my parents were able to travel and so the cards moved further afield. About this time too, my father gave up the trying work of the linocuts and switched to reproductions of pen and ink sketches. And so I see a page of pen-sketched band players from Petticoat Lane and the rooftops and sky of Bellinzona. The pen gave the cards a new grace and fluidity and I pause for a long while over my favourite, the arched interior of Ste Chapelle du Palais, with ornamentation streaming like rain over the lovely windows and arches.

Once again the focus changes. My parents began to visit us in eastern Ontario and liked what they saw. As always, the liking showed up in pictures, and I find an eastern Ontario log barn among the cards. Finally I am at the last pages and I find a card of the stone house near Yarker where they moved to be closer to the country and their family. The road is inviting and geese are beating overhead.

A print of the last card hangs over my desk. It shows a sweep of road running onwards around curves and over dipping fields. In it are a big sky, a snake fence and wind-shaped pines. Ironically, the eye travels first to a tiny roadside cemetery, but then sweeps quickly up and is caught by the perfect curve of a north-flying flock of geese. There is not one false line. Even more than all the cards of the portfolio it speaks of my father's profound delight in the beauty he found always and everywhere. By the time he drew it, his arthritis-twisted fingers balked at gripping the pen. Once, only once, he briefly mentioned that he no longer knew a time without pain. Yet the card rings out with an unparalleled joy in what he saw.

Bird nests in winter

Once the trees are bare and the pond ice hardens for easier access, I look forward to one of my favourite winter pleasures, the search for birds' nests. With the help of Hal Harrison's splendid *A Field Guide to Birds' Nests* (in the Peterson series) I prepare myself for a different way to appreciate birds. Although the migrants themselves are gone I feel a new intimacy with them after studying their homes.

This winter search is my reward for patience during the rest of the year. In spring I watched an apple tree, starry with blossoms and loud with bees. On its trunk is nailed a weathered bird house around which a pair of glossy tree swallows darted. As the season advanced, I kept my eye on the swallows' nesting place and on many others, imagining the unseen nests and hidden eggs, but also looking forward to winter when I could enjoy them without disturbing their occupants.

Only a few of the many nests in our area are visible before the leaves fall and of those I do discover, I would, of course, never disturb the occupants. For various reasons, some nests never will be accessible to me. In the case of the only nesting whippoorwill I ever encountered this was because she had formed no visible cup, but incubated her eggs on the forest layer of paper beech leaves. With a nesting family of pileated woodpeckers that I found in a tall, dead oak, it was because the large hole was thirty feet above my head. As

I visited the tree over the summer, I saw the heads of the three babies crowding out of the hole until at last they were fledged, but I wished the nest cavity had been lower so I could peer in to see the chamber the parents built for their young.

As I dip into Harrison's field guide, though, I am able to achieve a better understanding of what was going on, and an inspiration for the searching I do in winter. In the case of the woodpeckers, which did not return to the oak in the following years, I am relieved to learn that it is normal for them to build a new nest-hole annually. Also, I get a description of what I could not see, the inside of the cavity and a delicious anecdote about a female pileated who was photographed removing each of three eggs lengthwise in her bill from a destroyed cavity.

Perhaps being a weaver and a lover of baskets has something to do with it, but I find this book of nests charming and informative. It fills me with wonder that of the nests of two hundred and eighty-five species of birds recorded, no two look alike and each, to my taste, is a work of art. Take the five swallows included in the book, for instance. Each nest differs in its location, style or lining material. Before I can get out to examine the contents of the box in the orchard I learn that my tree swallows' nest is lined with feathers strategically placed so their curved tips curl over the eggs. Perhaps next year I'll remember that barn swallows usually incubate their eggs for about fifteen days so I will have a better idea of how long to expect our porch nest to be occupied. While I am on the swallow page I see that as many as fifty-five swallow nests have been reported in one barn.

Armed with memories of summer and pictures I have seen in the field guide, I make trips to find the nests that were hidden in the greenery all summer. How could I have missed the mud and grass cup of a robin's nest on the branch overhanging our lane? Yet it never fails to surprise me that, with the best of intentions, I can have missed so much. At last I am able to find the hanging, cradle-like nest of the oriole we knew was living in our cottonwood trees. Wetlands are among the best of places for bird watching; the little marsh nearby holds many bird homes. With a winter casing of ice, I can explore the swamp's interior as I never can in summer. Knee-high in the cattails I see the folded cattail nests of red-winged blackbirds. Nearby is the delicate woven cup of the American goldfinch, lined with thistle and cattail down.

After only an hour in the back field, pond and woods' edge I have come upon thirteen nests, some old friends, others, like the lacy fabrication of lichens and twigs that I found above my head in an oak, a new challenge for identification when I return home.

The house on Indian Hill

On the Sunday before Christmas I went house hunting on the road back of Indian Hill. The light was the thin, clear light of winter and the snowless fields were shrouded in a lingering frost.

I had come to Indian Hill looking for a deserted house. In my childhood there had been many abandoned houses. I had loved to explore them, playing at slipping into other lives as easily as I squeezed through paneless windows. Now such houses were rare, so I had been pleased when a friend had mentioned the Indian Hill place. "I haven't been over to it for a few years," Jim said, "but I think you'll find it more interesting than most. I don't know why it was, but when the last people there left, they left an awful lot of stuff behind. When you go in, it looks as if people were still living there."

I liked the old stone house right away. It sat well back from the road on the brow of a low hill. I followed the long, maple-lined driveway and as I approached it I pretended I was coming as a caller. There was a solid front door, generous enough, as were the best pioneer doors, for a coffin to pass out. Finding it firmly locked, I went around the side and stepped down to the cellarway. Here the stairs were thick with old crockery. I looked through a stack of saucers of blue and white, jonquil and roseware patterns. Next to them lay an old granite-ware egg poacher. There was no way to get in through the cellar, though. The heavy door had caved in, making a formidable barrier of rubble.

At last I found one door that positively invited exploration. I unlatched the screen door to the back kitchen and stepped into a home of the 1930's. Some houses I had investigated had seemed in a state of hopeless despair, bereft and waiting for inevitable decay to bring them to their knees. But here was a house that had been left forever as if the family might return to it. As I walked from room to room over the cold linoleum, it seemed as if life could be taken up at any minute.

I pushed up a curtain hiding shelves and found rows of preserve jars, the contents, age-darkened, but still sealed. From the clothes-line strung in the kitchen, a scarecrow collection of clothing dangled. Sentimental calendar pictures were tacked to the walls. As I lifted latches and pushed open doors, the sense grew on me that this had been a house of good cheer. The different papers on each wall had peeled in ragged strips, but each was bright and gay. Even the attic had sheets of newspapers pasted up and varnished.

The house had been one where children had played. Pairs of old, twin-bladed strap-on skates lay in corners. Assorted balls rolled over the uneven floors at the slightest nudge and marbles spilled out of a leather pouch on a horsehair sofa. In one room a rag doll lay on the floor, her insides shredded by mice.

In an overstuffed plush chair was piled a heap of tangled paper Christmas chains. The heavy curtains moved stiffly at a momentary breeze through the open kitchen door and I caught myself wondering when the family would be home. Perhaps even now they were leaving church with their heads full of Christmas. Up the broad front staircase was a bedroom with twin brown-enamelled iron bedsteads draped with cheap, frilly party dresses – a daughters' room, perhaps. I went to the broad-silled window and looked out across the fields, imagining the family's return.

For a brief time the humanness of this house had been such that I had been tricked into a sense of homecoming. But in truth I knew that the life of the house was nearly over. The air inside was brittle and cold. Jim had mentioned that the farmer thought of pulling down what he saw as a fire-trap in the new year. Out the window a cloud was crossing the pale sun and a flurry of snow slanted across the ploughed fields. It was time to leave.

The black buck

Surfeited with comfort and good cheer and jaded by the acquisitive chatter of overexcited children, I slipped on my coat, buckled on my snowshoes and headed for the woods. It was Christmas Eve in the afternoon and I was hoping to see deer.

How ironic it is that at Christmas one is often farther than usual from the very reverence this festival represents. Although I knew from certain heart-shaped tracks I'd seen and from the way our dog sniffed the air that the deer had returned to the park for the winter, I had let myself become more and more entangled in celebratory preparation and unintentionally I had become remote from the world that meant most to me. By Christmas Eve I realized that if I didn't get out of doors Christmas would lose its meaning for me this year.

I knew exactly where to go. Every year, whatever the conditions, the deer herd followed the same sequence. In fall they lingered deep in the woods, but by December they had moved to the area near what we called the Farm Pond, the beaver pond closest to the house. If we look out at dawn we sometimes see a ghostly band of them skirting the edge of our field. At night we often hear the crunch of their walking nearby.

I cut across the field, pushed my way through the junipers and came upon the evidence I was looking for. Pressed into the snow were three large oval depressions, the marks where three deer had been resting, curled up to conserve warmth. I bent and placed my hand in one of the forms. Very occasionally I came on one that still held warmth. This one was cold, but it was thrilling just to touch this sign of life in the midst of so much blank whiteness.

I remained by the lying down places simply enjoying the sun and the shadows that the surrounding thickets cast on the fresh snow. I drank in the cold, clear air and began to lose the heavy feelings I had brought with me from home. It was only a few days after the solstice yet I imagined I could already feel the sun's power strengthening.

A few minutes later I looked up from the delicate shadows to see the most splendid of all our deer standing calmly staring at me almost within touching distance. The huge black buck who appears to us only once a winter stood so close I could see his breath streaming from flared nostrils. He stood like a medieval symbol. One side of his antlers had fallen already, but he carried the other rack with all the dignity that monks gave to deer in early Christian paintings where they bore antlers in the shape of a cross. At a time when other deers' coats would have greyed to blend with the winter background, this one's was still a burnished red, darkened by much more black than is usual. Generally, animals that stand out are the first to die, yet this canny old buck had lived to become something of a local legend.

More cunning than any of the younger deer, he allowed himself to be seen only when he wanted to be. I knew he had appeared because of curiosity, but I felt moved because I believed he knew I was no predator. I was sure that, over the winters that we had paced the same back ridges and frozen ponds, he had often watched me, though I saw him seldom, and he knew, I thought, that I posed as little threat to his kingdom as another deer. And so we stood in a silence charged with understanding, and, on my part, with awe. Then he walked by me with weighted steps that cut deep into the snow and so disappeared into the woods.

The buck was gone, though I heard him and other deer moving in the forest and it was time for me to leave the woods. But now I felt that I could go home looking forward to the boisterous pleasures of Christmas and still more to the adventures out of doors that the new year would bring.

Owling at dawn

At six on Boxing Day morning, our door creaks with the cold and I step out into the hushed snowy world before dawn. At first there is no sound. Last night's stormy wind has stilled, leaving, as my stumbling feet describe, sculptured ridges and dunes of snow to block the lane. The moon has forsaken the sky, the stars are dim and fear edges in on me. It is Bird Count morning, and I have set out to listen for and call the great horned owls who lurk by the pinewoods bordering our fields.

I try to comfort myself with an image of many observers going forth from as far away as the Northwest Territories and the Panama Canal. For, within a two week period at Christmas, thirty-one thousand people will spend at least eight hours each ranging familiar haunts on foot and in car. Some of us will return saddened by diminishing numbers or the disappearance of beloved species. (There will be stories of counts that can no longer take place because beloved habitats have been bulldozed entirely.) Some will boast new sightings; all of us welcome the chance to share in forming the massive bank of data created by the "Annual Christmas Bird Count".

However, in the loneliness before dawn there is slight room for cheer. As each step persuades me that something sinister stalks my heels, my fear of looking back and confrontation heightens, until a wayside tree booms with the frost. I whirl, to face only emptiness and ghostly quiet.

Timidly, I cup my hands to my mouth and hoot seven times for the pair of owls who've haunted our fields of late. Many nights, driving home along the lane at dusk, I have seen them glide, as shadows to shadows, across my path. I've heard their muffled calls shifting over the snowy field and counted them hopefully for our part of the bird list. But on this lonely, important morning will they materialize in our part of their territory? If they are nearby, will they trouble to answer such a halting imitation?

To my surprise, with my call the fear in the darkness ends. I have made my mark and am placed within the scheme of things. When some deer crash and snap their way through the nearby woods, I merely hoot again and pause, then trudge along confidently. I am still navigating largely by sound and the feel to my feet of the drifted ruts. It is a lurching, easy rhythm, which makes me wonder how necessary sight is. Now that I have shaken the certainty and warmth of our house, and the fear of the unfamiliar world outside which followed it, I find the senses of balance, sound and touch more useful. Listening is particularly necessary, as I find that even the noise of my boots on the snow dulls my hearing and starts me imagining again, so that each frequent pause to let sound reach me gives me a grip on reality.

Through the breathless clarity of winter air I proceed until, at my next halt and cry, I turn back to the east and am held still a moment by a wash of palest light that has tinted the sky.

Almost, I am disappointed to see the dawn approaching steadily, making my world familiar again. To widen the territory I cover, I turn off the lane into a trail that skirts the meadow; even here, I can see dimly between the trees to make my way. The woods snow is soft and deep, so I must hitch my snowshoes on before I start. While I hunch to coax the stiff bindings around my boots, through the dawn woods I hear the seven throaty hoots of a great horned owl, followed by the rougher returning sound of a second, from a more distant point. Pierced, I straighten, call and am frozen by the closeness and malevolence of the answer I receive. No wonder the small mice and rabbits are driven to give themselves away when they hear this. I cannot decide which disturbs me more, the calls or the intervening silence. I remember the greatness of this owl and call no more. Soon their hooting fades, and the trees shift and crack in a stirring breeze, but I remain still, glorying in the powerful diminishing owl calls. At one point, the woods seems bubbling with owlishness.

I have succeeded in the predawn count; the owls are departed, and I see at length a brilliant red glow strengthening steadily among the trees. The deer are moving carelessly near the still-flowing stream that crossed the trail. Soon day birds will join them as the light heightens. Perhaps if I hurry I can reach the clearing as they appear. Drawn through the woods by the steady comfort of the dawn, I reach the meadow in time to hear a wonderful thing. A juniper tree beside me throbs with the secret sounds of small birds who had clearly spent the night there and are now stirring. Indeed, soft whistles and trills are everywhere as the sun clears the treeline, enabling me to see to jot down species and numbers. Already the owl song and the dim pre-dawn fears have grown dream-like.

Pleasant Valley

When I first read Louis Bromfield's *Pleasant Valley* my heart sang. I loved farms and the heritage and rhythm of farming. All around me I heard the story that farmers only farmed because they couldn't help themselves. The smart ones sold out; the others struggled on, each year further in debt, each year watching their poor farms become poorer. More than anything, I wanted to believe that sound farming was possible.

One snowy evening when I opened *Pleasant Valley* I read: "This book is a personal testament written out of a lifetime by a man who believes that agriculture is the keystone of our economic structure and that the wealth, welfare, prosperity and even the future freedom of this nation are based upon the soil.... It is, frankly, a romantic book, written in the profound belief that farming is the most honourable of professions and unquestionably a romantic and inspiring one." As I read, there came to me a wild hope that just possibly, with skill and careful husbandry, a worn-out farm could be restored to prosperity. Coupled with this was a renewed sense that this restoration was essential because agriculture was the backbone of us all. I began to look around me at the impoverished agricultural geography of my surroundings with renewed hope. It seemed that Louis Bromfield's love had wrought a practical example showing that the land could be healed.

He had bought three run-down Ohio hill farms, consolidated them and dedicated himself to the challenge of bringing back richness to the soil and renewing the forests. Writing with intense enthusiasm, he saw himself in the vanguard of what he hoped would be a new race of pioneers. Most importantly, he maintained and continued to maintain throughout his life, that Malabar Farm, (as the consolidated farms were called) was a demonstration of what could be done – done, he insisted, with no more money than the average farmer could raise.

Reading *Pleasant Valley, Malabar Farm* and *Out of the Earth*, I learned how in some places the land tripled its yield after he initiated organic farming procedures, how springs returned to irrigate the land, and the topsoil deepened. It was exactly what I wanted to hear and wanted to believe. As I read Bromfield, I dreamed of a similar greening of my surroundings.

I always planned that some day I would seek Malabar out. Sometimes I saw myself walking over the fields to Bromfield's favourite haunt, the wild and lovely Ferguson Place, which would look just as it had looked thirty years ago. In moods of doubt, I envisaged discovering a housing development replacing the pioneer farm.

Recently I chanced on "Malabar Farm Today" in a back issue of *Country Journal* and I faltered. Neither of my imagined Malabars was close to the truth. The farm continues, but as a "quiescent and attractive" state park run by the Ohio Department of Natural Resources.

Apparently Bromfield, rich from a series of successful novels, was able to buy the best equipment and afford to take risks. He never repaid his original investments and no one since has been able to make the farm profitable. Now it is run as a living museum. At the time of the 1977 article, however, it was not a museum that reflected Bromfield's beliefs. Atrazine was used to keep weeds down, and the friable soil was ploughed deeply with a mouldboard plough, two practices he strenuously opposed. As the author of the article drove through the surrounding countryside, he found that in fact no one had adopted Bromfield's conservation-minded methods. No one could afford to.

At first my feelings were all of loss. It seemed Bromfield's ghost had been laid along with the legend of Malabar. I reread my favourite chapter of *Pleasant Valley*, "My Ninety Acres", the heart piece of his writing, and thought that in it he had written his own epitaph: "There isn't anybody who will ever farm that earth again as if it were the only woman he ever loved." Even the larger-than-life Bromfield had failed in his quest to renew the land. But yet, the dream persists, too precious to let go.

Whenever I look at our exhausted fields, in my mind's eye I see Malabar as it was. For all Malabar's impracticability, we cannot afford to abandon Bromfield's dreams of renewal of the land.

At home till the end

Anna and I were sitting together in the old community hall listening to the fierce winter wind sucking the woodstove damper and sorting yarn before the weaving class gathered. "That's pretty," she said, taking up a skein of shocking pink: "I made a sweater that colour when Dad was living with us."

"There was a while when we didn't keep him, you know. It's hard, having an old man with you all the time. He got to bossing the kids a lot, and it wasn't fair on them. They had to be so quiet all the time. They couldn't even have any of their friends in. Finally, I just told him we couldn't do it anymore. And so he left. He was always a proud man, see.

"Well, we didn't hear of him for near two years. I didn't like it, but he didn't come round and we were busy with the store and the kids. At last my brother in Ottawa, he had Dad put in the hospital up there. Now, he could have kept Dad – he had plenty of money. But his wife Vera, she always wanted things so neat. She didn't want Dad because he was a bit sloppy on account of he didn't see too well – let ashes fall and that sort of thing.

"So then I went up to see Dad, and you know I wanted to sit on his bed and cry and cry. He just sat in bed in that white smock thing they wear and stared at the wall. He never even looked at me. But all I said was 'Dad, you're coming home with us again. You get your bag ready and I'll be up for you tomorrow.' He hadn't shaved, and I had never seen him not shaved before, so I got his kit and propped him up, and then I went out in the hall and found the doctor. Doctor thought I was crazy to take on all that work. But I knew I couldn't feel right with my Dad sitting up there in Ottawa all by himself."

Anna piled her tightly wound balls into the yarn box and walked over to the stove to stir the logs.

"How was it, having your father at home like that?" I asked.

"Well, he wasn't what he had been, and that made it both easier and harder too. The kids were real good. They were older by then and I think they were proud to have him. I know if Roger had an argument with us or trouble at school he went and sat with Dad a while. I don't know what they talked about, but when he came down again he'd be a lot easier to be around.

"Dad had to have a catheter then, and some people would say that's why he should have been in hospital. But the nurse showed me how to manage and he could strap the bag on his leg and get around real good. After a while his heart bothered him, and he just didn't have the same interest and then it was harder, the washing him and all.

"But you know, the hardest thing was the last morning he lived. I still don't know if I did right. In the night he was taken bad. He was in great pain and he was scared, and I was scared too, so Jack called the doctor and he wanted to get Dad into hospital. And then Dad looked at us, in all his pain and said he wouldn't go. He knew he was dying, and this was home now, and he didn't want to go. The doctor said he'd be better there, more comfortable, but I couldn't let Dad go. He kept saying he didn't want to go and I couldn't let him.

"After a little while the doctor left and Dad became very quiet, and then that was all. I used to think that when people died there was always a struggle, and I feared that, but Dad, he just slipped away quiet."

Anna and I sat silent in the warmth of the hall, and after a while she said, "I sent Dad away once because I thought it was hard on the kids having him with us, but in the end it meant more to them even than to me. Oh, yes, I'd advise anyone to keep their folks at home if they could."

Insects and domesticity

When cold weather comes to stay I miss the life that insects give to the outdoors, and by January I have almost forgotten stings and bites. I'm half-ashamed to admit it, but we actually hunt out and cultivate some of the insects that flourish all winter in our old house.

It all started with a dab of warm syrup that fell from a knife that was sticky from cutting into a hot apple pie. A few of the big, dazed wasps that linger on our porch in autumn invariably find their way into our house. We used to take a dim view of wasps, with their talent for relentless attack and multiple stings. The intruders usually ended meeting up with a fly swatter, an ignominious death for a wasp. Then, on a night so bitter that no houseplant bloomed and the only sound was a rugged wind tearing at the back of the house, one wasp resurrected itself and careened around the kitchen. Suddenly it took aim and plummeted onto a knife dripping with fragrant, warm pie juice and proceeded to feast. We watched him, fascinated by such an intimate view of an insect we usually avoided. Eventually Morgan went for a hand lens and we all peered at the striped body. What if we put out honey on a spoon and fed it like a pet? Jeremy suggested. The wasp-feeding venture succeeded, and that was how the wasp and several friends came to spend their winter in our kitchen. The gentle, stupid insects let us stroke them and study them all winter until the first day the crocuses opened wide when we let them fly off dizzily into the spring sun.

Since then we've made sure that we were well-supplied with wasps each fall. Granted, an unfortunate misunderstanding once lead to a sting on Jeremy's bare foot and one less wasp, but in general these over-wintering wasps have been excellent company.

Wasp watching has made me more appreciative of other insects in our house. In our kitchen window sat a pot of basil with stems encrusted with green aphids. Although I knew I should be treating the plant, I kept postponing the unpleasant job. When I finally decided to do something about the aphids, I was surprised to find that very few remained. As I searched for them I discovered a two-spotted ladybug moving decisively over its stems. From then on the ladybug and the aphids and the basil lived together without my intervention.

I know perfectly well that I ought to discourage the crickets who linger through the winter in our cellar; I know Barry is right when he warns me that they will eat the bags of fleece I have stored there. Yet, in order to hear fragments of their summer's end song, I turn a blind eye to the odd black figure I see scuttling for cover and I spurn boys who suggest that a sprightly cricket would make interesting food for our pet skunk Fanny.

With most of our insect residents we have no trouble. Like the ladybugs and the aphids they co-exist in relative harmony. About clothes moths, the other eaters of fibres, I can find little good to say, although out of self-defense I've made a pretty detailed study of their habits. With clothes moths I carry on a dark and subtle feud, using every weapon I can find, from freezing to herbal remedies. Perhaps the only value I can find in these spoilers is as providers of feline entertainment on long winter nights when the cats are bored to desperation. The wide-eyed pursuit of a moth provides them with welcome relief.

As I sit at my desk I glance up to see a diminutive spider waving its legs to add to the strands that already festoon the ceiling. I find it particularly difficult to destroy my fellow weavers, and I'm sorry to say all too many corners of my house sport their accomplishments. I should be thinking of fly swatters and brooms, but instead I can't help watching the grace of the spider and its web, echoed by the larger shadow spider and web on the wall. In winter each tiny fragment of life becomes newly precious.

Snowbound is fine

There comes a morning each winter when we wake to a muffled world where last night's snow continues to fall in floods. There is really no need to listen to the radio for school bus cancellations. We only have to look at the driveway to know we are snowbound, and what I want to say is that, as far as we are concerned, snowbound is fine. For one day at least, we are wrapped in snow, a rolling oceanish kind of snow that makes all the problems of the outside world mercifully remote.

"Aren't you afraid?" "Don't you feel isolated?" people ask. It's not like that at all. When I look out into the blurring snow I am exhilarated. Instead of feeling cut off I feel I am cutting back briefly into the things that really matter. Today, at long last, there will be time to read, to tinker on the piano with the Fauré that has been eluding me all month, to play with the boys. A snow day is a day to turn inward.

The radio confirms what we already know: there will be no

school or work today. The boys whoop. The rabbit, sensing she will have company in her kitchen today, does a rabbit ballet around the house, ending with a leap right onto my feet. There is nothing like the unexpected grace of a free day.

"Did you know we are almost out of bread?" asks Barry. It is now that our fall food storage pays off. I'm sure that, if pressed, we could live handsomely for at least a month before we would begin to run out. I head into the cellar which is dimmer than usual because of the hoods of snow over the windows, and scoop flour from the sack into my bread bowl. What better thing could there be to do on a snow day than to make bread?

As soon as breakfast is over the boys make the first of many trips out to play in the snow. By afternoon little trails of snow water will lead to a clothes rack dense with sodden clothes, but no matter. The joy of snow is too infectious for me to bring out the usual re-proaches. Instead I loiter, kneading my bread and watch out the window as monstrous snowballs wind their way past the window, shouldered forward by their creators.

After lunch I make a cup of tea and settle into a book on ferns, an apt antithesis to the white seas around us. I rummage through the pages, admiring lacy ferns, dense ferns, translucent, silver and gold ferns, and it comes to me that a cascade of ferns down one living room wall would be an excellent thing.

The day moves on, illuminated by the snowlight, and I feel more than ever that I am not confined, but rather am bound more closely to the people and things I love. Barry practices the piano and turns from time to time to show me an exciting new bit he's found. The boys sit on the floor working on favourite old puzzles. Meanwhile, the flakes that fall past the window are getting bigger, lazier, "like feathers," Morgan says.

An hour before evening, I notice that there is a different quality in the light. When I put the steaming bread on the table to cool, I can see a touch of orange in the western sky and I find myself feeling almost sorry the snow is ending. There's a stirring clarity in the air, however, and we all begin to be drawn back to the outside world again.

"We'd better get up early tomorrow," says Barry. "I'll want to get the trails packed before my class comes in."

"I wonder if Randy will be bringing his toboggan to school tomorrow?" says Jeremy.

While the soup simmers, we leave the house to explore the new snowy world before the light goes. Tomorrow we'll be glad to hear the plough trundle down the driveway, but today we will walk over the trackless snow, tasting the last happiness of our snowbound day.

Valentine

Valentine. As I am putting down his name, a clumsy, big Siamese pads into my room, stretches to an amazing height in order to peer out the window, flips down, pads over to my chair and, with a heavy leap, is in my lap. With only a sketchy attempt at a purr, for Valentine is chary with his purrs, he settles into a rich winter cat sleep. As my pen moves, his cool, steady breath crosses my hand.

More than our other cats, he is an enigma. We do not know his past and sometimes (his sides are heaving just now with one of his rare nightmares) even now he is not ours. Four years ago in February, our kind friend Lil Dodge phoned. She knew we had lost our first Siamese the previous October and she had come across a replacement at the Humane Society. He was three years old and she knew we'd wanted a kitten, but he was beautiful and he was stuck in a cage over a retriever that was barking incessantly. Could she bring him to us?

Coming to us as he did on February 14, it was inevitable that he became "Valentine" and when we read his Humane Society card with "Name-Valentine" written on the bottom, the coincidence did not even surprise us. But we knew little else about this handsome, brown stranger at first, for his card gave us only his age, name and the date of his shots. Watching him those first February days, we realized what a shock our life must have been to him.

Although he was not wilful, he sauntered across tables and snatched at food with such confidence that we had to assume that he had never been disciplined before. From the way his eyes became saucer-wide when our boys roared through the house, we deduced that he was not used to children. Worst of all, apparently he had never experienced other cats and now he was confronted by a pair of jealous dowagers, grimly determined to make him (and us) pay for this intrusion. For a month we waited as "the girls" hissed and recoiled with horror as this meekest of cats edged past them in hallways. With his bulk he could easily have cuffed them to submission. Instead, he withdrew. We began to fear we had made a mistake. It had been unfair to the old cats to introduce a stranger and doubly unfair to Valentine to bring him to such an alien home. Then one day I caught Small curled up with Valentine looking at me sheepishly, and a few nights later Morgan found the three curled in bed together. (After all, big cats do generate more heat.) He's always remained a little apart from them, but he has been accepted.

We think he must have known love with his first owner. Before long he forgave our noise and threw himself whole-heartedly into being a people cat. Unlike the other two, who retire when the going gets rough, he is happiest wherever we are. He has pushed himself into my heart as a would-be weaver, spinner, breadmaker and ardent walker. If I go downstairs to the washing machine, I hear a yowl and look up to see Valentine peering down moonily from the heat ducts. When we sit on the couch, he wedges himself between us. If the boys play baseball, he is in the thick of the game.

Valentine. The clues to his past are so few, this much-loved cat who spreads himself heavily on my knee. He's ours now, but one small trick reminds us that his past was not ours. Once, Jeremy passed by with a crust of bread held low and he sat up like a little dog and pirouetted, begging. Someone, somewhere had taught him and played with him. The silly little trick had mattered to this unknown person, and then, for some reason, the owner had left him and his life had changed.

Once in a while the boys get him to repeat his trick and the dignified, little-old-man cat waltzes around to the tune somebody else taught him. As I watch him make his circle I think of then and now and the changes he's come through.

And then, and then and then

Did you ever, as a small child, have one of those days at school where one thing after another went wrong? By two-thirty you thought the day would never end, and three-thirty saw you thrust your nose through the classroom door on the "D" of "Dismiss" to run all the way home, panting and huffing chokily every step of the way. Very likely you stubbed your toe or perhaps even skinned your knee, but at last you burst in the door, and, before your mother could ask, "What sort of day did you have, dear?" you recounted all the miserable, unfair things that had happened to you in a flood of "And then, and then, and then..."

It's been an "and then, and then, and then" sort of day around here today since noon, when we learned that a cherished piece of wild land must be sprayed with defoliant. The old, infuriating feeling of helplessness came back as vividly as if I had just come out of school.

"It won't be so bad," Barry said. "They'll be spraying a long way from houses. At least it won't affect people at all. Just the trees in the way will die." But I said quickly, "What about the woodpeckers? They love that sunwarmed hillside, and they'll be after the bugs when those trees die." He didn't deny it.

And then I thought of the predators that might eat an insect-poisoned woodpecker. Great hawks might sicken and grow weak. A carrion eater, a fox perhaps, delighted to find a dead woodpecker, might return to its pup-filled den with an evening meal.

Or would it be more insidious? The red-tailed hawk who soared over the hillside might have no young to fill her nest next spring. A skunk might rip at the rotting wood with her delicate, curved claws, searching for and eating poisoned beetles.

And then I thought of the indigo bunting who came to the hillside each summer, a flash of exquisite blue against the dark, fern-like foliage of the sumacs. I had recently taken part in a bird census where we noted unusually large numbers of common species, but few rarities. This, I had read, often was a sign of pollution. Each year we saw fewer unusual birds. Who would keep the insect numbers manageable with them gone?

Because the woods below the hillside was so dense, it was rich with thrush song in June and with warblers. Perhaps we would lose not just the flashes of blue but the haunting song of the secretive thrushes as their woods opened up.

And then I saw the hillside in the heat of summer, the milkweed bent and scentless, mullein, rumpled and flabby, and, against the summer greenery, the rattling, stark dead leaves of the sprayed saplings. There would be no brush pile neatly made here that might have been a shelter for animals. The decay replenishing the frail hillside soil would be tainted. And for how long?

"Well, we'll just have to fight it," I said. "We've fought other things. Sometimes we've won. If they'd just give us time, men who need jobs could cut the brush. We must make them wait."

"You know, Barry said, "you could be taken to court for interfering too obnoxiously with a government agency."

After all, it was only a hill with woodpeckers and a waterfall. There would be other times with things we'd really have to fight for. And then I wondered, just how many losses will I accept before I do decide to fight back?

New life for an old basement

I should warn you that you probably wouldn't like our cellar. The cellar of an old country house is something the owner of a new house could not imagine and likely would not want to.

I've come a long way as far as basements are concerned. Ten years ago, after a week of living in a bricked-over pioneer log house, I investigated the basement our landlord had described as "not too much use." The smell from the musty earth floor alone should have been enough to drive me back, but curiosity got the better of me.

With only a flashlight to guide me, I walked warily across to what appeared to be an old cistern and tipped my light into it. To my disgust, the flashlight revealed a mass of sickly, elongated sprouts from unplanted dahlias and potatoes, clawing for a light they could never reach. I didn't wait to see more and I didn't return to that basement.

My current cellar and I got off to a bad start. The first time I set foot on its stairs, the members of a Rideau Valley Conservation Authority crew stood around outside snickering and teasing me. "Didn't I know there was a nest of black rat snakes down there? Boy was I going to be sorry." They told me they'd seen them down there just writhing around. With each stair I descended the count got larger until, when my feet touched the uneven cement floor, the number was up to a hopeful "maybe even forty of them or more." I'm fond of black rat snakes (king snakes, as they're sometimes called for their large size) and I know they are harmless, but I prefer meeting them on equal ground. The thought of raising my eyes to stare into the eyes of a large black snake hanging in the rafters did not encourage me. Still, I didn't want to lose face with "the boys" so I stayed down there and took my first look around. I think they did believe there were at least some snakes, but, because not one of them had ventured into the cellar before me, none of them could have known. Suffice it to say that I never then or later, found a single snake in our basement.

At first I did not find our cellar much more compelling than the dirt-floored one. I stumbled on the uneven, broken cement and cracked my head on the low beams. It was dim and musty, and who knew what could be lurking in its badly-lit corners? However, after long acquaintance, I've come to like our old country cellar for a variety of reasons. Now I find even the fact that it's close to the bone adds to its charms. Each time I descend the rickety stairs, the first thing my eye catches is one of the unpeeled cedar posts that support the first floor. I like to think of the man who cut them and wonder where on the property they came from and when. I tie bundles of drying summer everlastings to them and enjoy the simplicity of a time when a house was built from its surroundings rather than a lumberyard's truckload. The cement floor may be rough and cracked, but it smacks of a family building a home for themselves and self-reliance and I prize that more than the slickest, corporation-tiled floor. I even like the cracks themselves as a reminder that the house is set on earth, and, although a shelter for us, is a vulnerable, breathing, changing organism of its own.

As for that horrifying vision of the sickly, unplanted potato and dahlia shoots at the other house, we, too, have made this cellar a storage place for our winter food, and when I visit our bulkhead cold cellar or lift the lid of our freezer, this worn old basement becomes the heart of the house to me, filled with remembrances of summer bounty and promises for a safe winter.

Winter ponds

When winter sets in to stay and the water freezes hard I look forward to exploring our beaver ponds. Because their water is impassable for canoes, only in winter do I have this chance.

Many a prospective landbuyer has been disappointed to discover that the "small lake" a real estate agent advertised was really just the drowned land of a beaver pond. To a casual observer these "lakes" appear to be desolate, wasted land, but I've found through my winter prowlings that such a place is full of interest.

Last January I skied back to our "Bachelor Beaver's Pond", so-called because for some years it was the home of a solitary, crusty beaver. The preceding two winters, however, the lodge had been vacant. This is the pond that appears least interesting to a summer visitor. Unlike our other ones in the shade of the woods, it lies in a hollow of a field, shallow, and densely sheltered by scrub alders and willows. Even in winter this pond wards off visitors. So much brush surrounds it that thrusting my way in on skis was tough. In summer I had noticed a little, hard-packed animal runway leading into the pond and in the end I used this path to push my way through. Once I was within the willow and alder walls, the snow-covered spread of the pond seemed like a secret room.

First I turned to the wood duck house that is nailed to a dead elm. I lifted its lid and searched cautiously with my hand. As I had hoped, there were large, downy feathers mixed with the wood chips inside. Although I had not been able to see these most exotic-looking of our ducks the summer before, I was glad to know they had nested here and, in all likelihood, had raised a brood. I pulled out one airy, striped feather to take home with me.

The Bachelor Beaver's Pond has been a pond for a long time. Unlike the younger ponds, this one was almost an unbroken expanse of snow that was brilliant in the bright January sun. Few dead trees remained standing to break the surface, but where they were I saw several castor piles, territorial marks indicating that there now was more than one beaver living in this pond. Following the curve of the shore, I found the markings of fox and coyote as well. That January morning much could be read here. Only slightly more sophisticated than the castor piles were the conical muskrat houses that were mounded up among the cattails at the shallow end of the pond. I was beginning to get a picture of the summer life that would go on in this place.

As I skied around the pond, I caught more glimpses of the abundant life it sheltered in summer. Tucked into the low-growing bushes that walled in the pond I came across more birds' nests of many different kinds than I have found in any other single area.

At last I reached the beaver lodge. Very little had been added to it. It was barely a bump in the snow, but, yet, there was its frost hole, the ventilation hole between the branches where the warm air of a living animal had turned to frost crystals. I pulled off my glove and pushed in my finger to feel the warm air inside.

All was well there, so I recrossed the pond, following a deer track until I got to the fine new lodge that more recent residents had made. This lodge was much larger and bristling with fresh sticks. I found several frost places and then pulled off my skis and perched myself on the lodge to listen, an activity that is one of the high points of my winter.

I sat very still, staring at the hard, cloudless blue sky and the writing a broken reed made scraping back and forth across the snow in the wind, and I listened deeply. Soon I heard what I was waiting for.

From beneath me I heard little chirring sounds, then a splash, a second splash and a succession of rolling gurgles. Above my head, near the top of the lodge, some dried pearly everlasting flowers from last summer rustled in the breeze.

The pond, old though it was, was supporting more life than ever. I could go home in peace now, content to wait until next winter for the next chapter in the story.

Sally

Some rainy nights, when I lie in bed I hear the sump pump working in our basement, and I think of the water coursing and seeping around and beneath our house. On these nights I'm reminded of Beatrix Potter's excellent frog Jeremy Fisher and the water all "slippy-sloppy" in his passage. From Jeremy Fisher it's but a short leap to a special amphibian that appears to us only rarely and in wet seasons; the spotted salamander that presides over our cellar.

Often the sump pump sticks and on one such a night Barry ran down to release it. As the rush of water clicked off, he turned to find a salamander as long as his hand standing motionless behind him on the cement. In the dead of winter, diversions are welcome and Barry called me down to see what he had found. Sally, whom we arbitrarily decided was a she, perhaps because of a certain earth mother quality, stood silent and unyielding. Her four legs splayed out from her body and her rounded tail stuck out behind her. (Salamanders, Barry reminded me, are the only amphibians that keep their tails through their entire life.) We admired the yellow spots like painted jewels on her black back and I bent over and hesitantly touched them. We half-expected such a secretive, nocturnal creature to dart off, but Sally, as we've learned from further encounters, has a lot of poise and is not the darting type. Although she has none of a snake's scales, her body, like that of a snake, is smooth and dry rather than slimy. Touching her, I sensed something dim in her as if her life force had not completely kindled, and I remembered that her history as an amphibian goes back eons. In the shadowy cellar I touched her again and in slow-motion she extended one foot and stopped. Not wanting to disturb the salamander more, we soon went upstairs, leaving her standing mid-floor, like an ornamental household goddess.

The next time, it was Morgan who found her drawing herself leisurely out of a small hole in the concrete floor, and we were glad to know she was a permanent resident. Often after that the boys placed a choice insect by the hole, and it always disappeared. Old cellars are notorious as homes for a whole network of insects and I have no doubt that ours remains reasonably insectless largely because of Sally's efforts.

One day disaster struck. A Rideau Valley employee with some patching cement to seal cracks in the basement walls, saw Sally's hole and smoothed cement over it as well. When we came home from work and school we were horrified to find hardened cement. Hastily, Barry chipped away the hardened cement, but we had little hope that Sally had survived. But it takes more than cement to kill a salamander, and, amazingly, she reappeared that spring, as serene as ever.

In the meantime, with the arrival of the spring rains, I had been making the acquaintance of a relative of the spotted salamander, the red eft. Walking along the sandy road after a rainstorm, I saw efts, tiny (four or five centimeters) and coral-coloured. Very carefully, I picked up one of the sprightly little newts and carried it off to the side of the road, marvelling at its transparent, weightless body in the centre of my hand. The eft's story is like a fairytale. The red eft is the terrestrial stage in the development of the development of the red-spotted newt. For one to three years it is condemned to the land and then it matures and returns to the water for good. Like other salamanders it avoids sunlight, but bolder or less wary than most, it does appear during the day, especially in damp weather.

It's winter again now, and below me the water sluices and rushes in the pump. It is likely that that primitive, painted creature walks, more slowly than slow, is stalking some sow bug or cricket. Soon I'll sleep again and tomorrow she'll not be there. But perhaps when I send our Jeremy down to the basement for a bag of apples he'll see wet salamander toe-prints and the dragging trail of a tail.

Cabin fever

Cabin fever. It usually attacks me in February about the time I've been stuck in the house for a week with a sick child and have been kept in a further week by storms into which only the foolhardy would venture out. At last comes a day of brilliant sun and yet I shuffle my feet at the door and hesitate with all the enthusiasm of a swimmer faced with frigid water. I'm longing to break out, but I've lost touch with the wintry world that has remade itself in my absence. What I see is a harsh blue sky unrelieved by so much as a cloud and a landscape softened by so much snow that it appears to be a sea of undefined whiteness.

Gingerly, I poke my nose out the door and am confronted by air of a purity I'd forgotten could exist. At my back is the dark, musty atmosphere of the house. After two weeks of exile from the out of doors my prison has become familiar to me, though, and I approach this now-foreign world with hesitation. I will have to use snowshoes for my breakaway. Skiis are fine for gliding over open spaces and well-groomed trails, but for my favourite backwoods terrain of rocks, thickets and hummocks I need the freedom that snowshoes give me. Turning my mind firmly away from the futile thought that only a few months before I had walked lightly and at will through the park, I fumble with the frozen bindings. How different are these rough, sturdy snowshoes from my mother's elegant, handmade pair which I used when I first came to the country, yet both pairs have taken me on fine adventures. I work my boots into the bindings, tighten the straps, and am ready to set off. As I prepare to go, I try to find my bearings in this air so clear it threatens to crack. My feet, quicker to adapt than my will, soon regain the rolling easy gait the shoes require and take the waves of snow in their newfound stride. How strange to think that at thigh- or maybe even waist-depth below the snow-skimming shoes waits the world that will be spring. The lichen- and moss-covered granite, the roots and seeds of grass and field flowers, the mice in their grassy nests: all they lack now is the earth's turning.

At the edge of the woods I pick up and follow a well-travelled deer path that heads in a wandering fashion towards the eastern ridges. Many times I've walked what I thought was aimlessly through the woods, only to find I had been following a deer path without knowing it. Whether this means my mind works like that of a deer, or that deer in their wandering find ideal paths through rough country, I can't say. Thinking along these lines about the minds of deer and their ways, I am brought up sharply against one deer fact – their limited height – when a low-hanging branch across the trail whips my face.

Breathless I prop my back against one of the lightning-stunted oaks of the ridge and look far to the east through branches that in summer will be shuttered with leaves. I'd forgotten how matchless views in winter are. I'd forgotten oh, so many things about winter. I'd forgotten the quiet, and the surprisingly warm silence that brings one close to the things that matter. I'd forgotten that the country never feels more like your own private domain than when seen in February whiteness.

Our resident flock of sixty cedar waxwings whistles past me and lands to ornament a nearby bare-branched tree. Ahead of me my deer trail leads down a steep hill to a whole system of beaver ponds. The air is still sharp but once more I am back outdoors where I belong. Turn back to the house? Not a chance.

The third meeting in four days

We were on our way to our third meeting in four days on a March night some years ago. There were knots in both our stomachs as we began to rehearse questions and points. As usual, there was no time for real conversation, just the facts. Rain was streaming over the car windows, but it was real rain, not snow.

Just after the campground hill, the headlights picked up a brownish shape plodding towards us and Barry stopped. "Peri, it's a beaver, for heaven's sake." The beast paused beside the car, dazed, and, meeting forgotten, we rolled down our windows and looked. Tiny ears, rain-sodden fur, paddle tail – we were captivated looking at this first beaver of spring, so very far from any pond. After a few minutes he set off down the road again. "You know what we're seeing, of course," said Barry. "That must be one of the two year olds. He's been driven out by his mother. She'll soon be having kits again. Now he's on his own and looking for a new home." I thought of the nearer ponds, of the fine, empty lodge at the Farm Pond, and the hopelessly shallow pool where a doomed youngster had thrown together a sketchy shelter another year. "Let's follow him," said Barry, meeting forgotten. "We're not likely to get another chance like this." My eyes followed the beaver, but I had to say it, "We have a meeting to make." The car started and we set out for Brockville, but on the long drive I felt rebellious.

Meeting going begins with pride, I've noticed. I started out tossing off "I've got a meeting tonight," importantly. As soon as I was pinpointed as a willing attendant, my activities expanded. Before I knew it, I was out two or three nights a week. At my next function, I began to look around the table. Most present looked overworked and exhausted. There was much talk of "It takes a busy person to get things done." As the evenings dragged on it seemed accomplishments came painfully slowly and there was no time to talk to my neighbours and hear the truly important things. I did hear the group decide to go after S. for missing three meetings in a row, but I did not get to ask how J.'s mother was making out after her operation.

That night I decided that a second career of meetings was not for me. I believe in civic duty, but long for the kind of democracy where all take pride in taking turns with this duty. Thinking it over, I've found three classes of get-togethers I can do without. First to go are tea-party meetings, leaning heavily towards elaborate eats and close-to-the-bone gossip. Along with them I decided to toss out fact-and-figure meetings which allow little input. I'll read a synopsis later. Most insidious are parent groups such as Friends of the Junior Ballet and Hockey Mothers. Parents are often coerced into these with the cry "It's for our kids", but I'll be glad when they realize that most of our kids are not little professionals. They should do what children are supposed to do to learn to be grown up: play. They can and should play at swimming, gymnastics, drama and hockey with very little adult intervention. I've come to distrust any child-centred venture requiring elaborate costumes, uniforms or equipment and I'm suspicious of parents who get entangled in too many of these activities. Are they really doing it "for the kids"?

When we returned home that night at eleven-thirty, the rain had stopped and the beaver had gone. We had won our point after a strenuous fight, but we did not feel victorious. Neither side had been wrong. Both were confronting a lack of government funding. We remembered the bitter, disappointed faces of parents who stood to lose not as much as we did, but more than enough. Also, we remembered the lost beaver in his watery landscape and how we'd had to turn our backs on him. I can't say there will be no more meetings, but before I go to another, there will have to be a good reason.

Grog's story

Grog's story begins with fleeting glimpses of a nondescript young mongrel loping across a frozen field near Leamington. When three-year-old Morgan and I went for walks, we watched a wild-looking dog, and, furtively, he watched us. Like an animal from the *Just So Stories*, over the next month he slunk closer to our house. We caught his wolf-ish eyes staring at us from a ditch, from a shed, from a cornfield. Like a Kipling animal he moved in gradually and ingratiated himself.

One morning I looked out to check on Morgan, whom I had left wandering forlornly in the lonely yard. Any minute now I expected him to stump back up the stairs, demanding to come in, but wait, there was the dog standing by Morgan and wagging his tail. I held my breath, ready to intervene, but Morgan, with a new companion, was happy to stay outside.

Over the next few days I kept a close eye on the two. They played like puppies, sniffing and rummaging everywhere. The new friend was lean and appeared promptly whenever I let Morgan outside, but I assumed he had a home. At least, I did until one day when we went for a walk with the dog slinking along too, at a safe distance. Hardly believing my eyes, I saw him raid a corn crib and devour some frozen cobs. After a week of watching him tear at the frozen corn I broke down and bought him a bag of dog food. However, he was not, I warned Barry and Morgan, going to become our dog. I appreciated his support with Morgan, but the food was as far as my thanks would go.

Then came the accident. One rainy March evening a car flashed past, and before Grog knew it, he'd been hit. Barry ran to help but the dazed dog apparently believed that somehow he was responsible for the maddening pain in his side. Panicking, he plunged away across the muddy field. "You try," Barry suggested to me. "He still trusts you." I squelched through mud almost to my boot-tops until I found the dog cowering against a distant fence. He was muddy and bloodstained, but the pain in his eyes spoke of what he saw as a second betrayal. When he refused to come with me I had no choice. I hefted him up and struggled home to our basement with him.

On cleaning him, I found his wound was superficial. Something in his patience touched me as well as the cock of his ears and the warmth of his eye. When the graze on his side healed I had to remind myself that we couldn't take on a dog. Grog understood. He had been respectful but uneasy in the house. Plainly he was relieved to be outside again.

In June we gave in. We were moving to Kingston and somehow, in spite of our early resistance and without any formal discussion, it was agreed that Grog would be coming too. We were bringing him for Morgan, we said.

Then, just when Grog's future seemed brightest, something went wrong. As the pile of packed boxes mounted he became listless and began to stagger. I took him to a vet who diagnosed distemper. The day before we were to leave, Barry tried another vet. Grog had epilepsy, this one told us. Pills might help, but it was likely he was dying. The next day I set Grog on the back seat of our car beside Morgan and started on the long drive to eastern Ontario. I had no doubt that Grog, who had fought so gamely to survive and be accepted, was dying and I couldn't help him.

It was late when we reached our new home, and Morgan, eager to explore his new surroundings, burst open his door. But, could it be? There, right behind him was Grog, not a fading, wavering dog, but Grog of the sly grin and plumy tail. This dog, better than new, explosive with happiness, raced madly around the new fields.

Unlikely as it sounds, I knew then that Grog had no physical illness. His sickness had been grief. He had known the signs. We were moving. Once before that had meant he was abandoned. He could not and would not face that again. Now in the dusk I heard Morgan calling and the dog's joyful barks. The stray had come home for good.

How did Grog the stray find his new life with us? An uncle once asked us "Don't you think your dog would be happier if he had a life like our Snoopy's? He gets so much more love and attention than Grog does." I thought of stout, immaculate Snoopy, living in a centrally air-conditioned home, going for ten minute walks where his paws never left concrete, guzzling expensive food and taking a variety of medicines prescribed by a slick city vet. Then I thought of Grog, our scraggy, bright-eyed, mostly border collie. I could answer only that it seemed like the town mouse-country mouse debate to me. Snoopy would never be happy away from his comforts, but then Grog... well, I could see Grog in the other house, meekly accepting the attention and the treats, but all the while his eyes would be growing cunning. One day, just once, a door would be left the least bit ajar and Grog, the rough, tough country dog would be headed out.

Part of the difference, and one of the things I like best about Grog is that he's nobody's pet. As far as he's concerned he has us; it's not the other way around. He's a survivor. Now, like all who've had to make their own way, he's independent and self-reliant.

And oh, how he loves his rough, lean way, Grog, the scourge of the groundhogs, Grog, the terrorizer of impertinent and alien trucks. When I think of him I see him snapping and tussling joyously with first one and then two boys. I hear the lusty sneezes as he mouses in the long grass. Then I see him running with banner ears. (Because he can't wait to get on with living, Grog is forever running.)

It's true that Grog does not enjoy the benefits of air conditioning. Instead, like any bad dog worth his salt, he wallows in the nearest pond, snorting and rolling his eyes like an alligator, then, dripping wet, he heads for a shady sandpile. As for food, Snoopy may well prefer his little cakes, but having watched the relish with which Grog tucks into vintage groundhog, I'm inclined to suspect it makes up for his dull, dry dog food.

"Trouble," I mutter, shaking my fist at Morgan, Grog's companion and ally. "That dog is nothing but trouble. Do you know how many times this makes that he's come home with a face full of quills? And in heaven's name why does he always get them evenings and Saturdays when the vet's office is closed?"

"Some dogs learn and some don't," the vet had said the third time Barry took him in.

"That makes ours one of the stupid ones," Barry had pointed out. But I don't agree. Grog is convinced that it is only a question of time until he will catch one of those hateful creatures off guard and then he will pay it back for every wrong it ever did to the dog tribe.

Grog is sure he knows best, and quills are only part of the price he pays for his independence. He has survived a bullet that passed clean through his abdomen, being clipped by a car, and a fight with a bull raccoon who shredded an ear and one with a beaver that tried to drown him. We expect at least once a year to hear the vet doubt that the dog with the wicked gleam in his eye will last the night. Grog has made as many last appearances as the Crummleses in *Nicholas Nickleby* and each time I've been taken in.

Time is getting on for even Grog now. In the past year his eyes have clouded, although he still gets around as well as ever. I have no doubt his bones and battle scars often ache, but his keen interest in life continues. Even the groundhogs don't lure him far from the house anymore, but he doesn't care. As long as he can herd the cats and the red squirrels and us he's satisfied. Would he trade places with Snoopy? Never!

•

In the end, even Grog could not go on forever. A few years after this was written he startled me one day by turning back from his walk. Sheepishly, he pretended he had taken a shortcut to get back in time to wolf Morgan's toast crusts. When it happened a second day, both of us knew something more was wrong, because no true country dog ever puts food before a walk. The vet told us the old dog had a tumour in his nose. With an understanding we'll always appreciate, he suggested we keep him at home with us for as long as he still loved life. And we did. That fall was tinged with sadness for us all. It wasn't easy staying by him in his bad times, seeing bouts of apathy and the dullness of pain. Yet, sharing his dignified path to the end taught us how much better animals bear suffering than do humans. He still wanted to live. Of that we were quite sure. To us, the shortened, slow-paced walks to the end of the driveway and back seemed pitiful compared to his former wide-ranging gallop, yet he plainly loved them. When he was uncomfortable, he endured, but he did not fear between times, but put himself wholly into the moment. In October the game was finally up. He'd had a hemmorrhage and we had phoned the vet to arrange to bring him in for the last time. That afternoon I took him for one final walk, willing with all my might that my sadness might not pass on to him. And yet, as Grog had always known things without them being said, he knew. On the walk out he moved with surprising jauntiness, yet within a minute after I headed him back home, he apparently took matters in his own hands; he always had been his own master, and so, it seemed, he chose his own time and place to die. This time the blood was unstoppable. By good fortune Barry had just finished with his class and could help me. By still better fortune a kind friend came by and ended the finished life quickly and cleanly with a bullet in the orchard where Grog had so often scented the wind. Because we had been with him to the end, we could not mourn. His death was entirely right. But, for many months afterwards, our house and the fields were much quieter.

Shotgun living

The best thing that ever happened to me was living for five months, in a modest sort of way, with the possibility that I might die at their end. For five months I lived in terms of a slim threat that my days were closely numbered. Before my eyes, life bloomed and became astonishingly desirable. The scent of bread, a baby's hands, a leaf tumbling across the grass, the first star, the simple, routine jobs I had resented, all enlarged themselves into gifts beyond price.

Yes, I felt regret too, but most of all, I kept saying to myself, "I never really noticed." When the long tomorrow suddenly threatened to shrink, I found my life scale shifted drastically. Getting ahead and being right fell into the shadows. Instead I found I was endlessly demanding of myself, "How could you have missed this? How could you have had so much and not been happy every day of your life?" It wasn't the dramatic things that impressed me. It was the common feelings like sitting in a chair in a pool of sunlight and hearing a robin through the open window that became unspeakably poignant when I thought I might never have them again.

At the end of my five months the odds were with me. I came through my operation safely and began to get used to the idea that I might, well almost, live forever. I tried to keep my new value for life, but as daily existence dulled the edge of it, I often recalled Flannery O'Connor's desperately funny short story "A Good Man is Hard to Find". In it she says a character would have been a good man if he could have been shot every day of his life. Since my brush with mortality I'm inclined to think that we all need a shotgun pointed at us to keep our appreciation of life at the fever pitch it merits.

Last spring I faced death in a different way as I visited my father-in-law in a cancer ward. I dreaded going. I imagined the suffering and sorrow would be profound. They were, but oddly enough, they were not what was important. As I sat in waiting rooms, walked the halls, talked to patients, and, most importantly, kept Dad company, what struck me was the fierce beauty of this life at the end of a gun. There was love such as I've never seen anywhere else, shiny pockets of love in the most unlikely places. In the hall I saw a hard-looking father and his slick, grown-up daughter laughing and teasing in common words, only their faces were lit with an uncommon love. In the dreary waiting room a pinch-faced nurse slipped up from another floor to spend coffee breaks with her dying young girl of a sister. I watched her devouring and memorizing the girl over and over with her eyes. (Oh, the luxury it would have been to her to know she could see that face for just one more year.) Everywhere dams were breaking and lifetimes of unspoken love were spilling out. Why does it take dying to let these out?

Thornton Wilder in his play *Our Town* has Emily say it all when, as a ghost, she looks back on the living:

> It goes so fast. We don't have time to look at one another…. I didn't realize. So all that was going on and we never noticed…. Goodbye to clocks ticking … and Mama's sunflowers. And food and coffee. And new-ironed dresses and hot baths … and sleeping and waking up. Oh, earth, you're too wonderful for anyone to realize you…. Do any human beings ever realize life while they live it? – every, every minute?"

And that is what Foley Mountain is all about, a place set apart where it is harder not to experience life fully. As I write another spring is racing towards us. Just last night the woodcocks came back. We heard their fluty calls when we stepped out to listen to the many waters pouring off the land. And the stars – there's something special about the stars on a misty spring night. And now today – Look over there … surely yes, it's the first marsh hawk gliding over the field. He's early this year.

Come on. What are we doing sitting inside here? Let's walk out where the snow is creeping off the fields. It's the beginning of a new year in the country and there's so much we have to see.

Afterword

Foley Mountain, October 1, 1994.

Much has changed and much has stayed the same.

Both of the beloved little boys who enlivened the pages of this book have widened their territories. Morgan, now twenty-four, has a Masters degree in History, and is training to be a teacher. Although he presently is living in a city out of necessity, the Canadian wilderness is deeply engrained in him. His dream is to build a cabin in the woods and live there. Jeremy, at twenty, is totally in love with Canada's largest city. He is in his second year of specializing in History and Medieval Studies, and suspects that eventually he too will follow his father and become a teacher.

Grog being an exceptional dog, it actually took four dogs to replace him. Joyously herding Barry and me on our walks are three small and plucky Welsh Cardigan corgis and Missy, the immense Irish wolfhound. For a few momentous years, through moments of weakness which I cannot explain, (Barry says I do not want to) our family of cats grew to five. After a rewarding life presiding over our kitchen, Bun, Morgan's sprightly grey rabbit, died of cancer at the age of five. It was typical of her vigorous spirit that even on her only visit to the Vet, to be euthanized, she, who once had been so timid about unfamiliar situations, and now was fatally ill, managed to entertain and hearten a whole roomful of families who were waiting in the office. Fanny, our skunk, lived a long life for a skunk, dying at eight, and we were shocked by how much we missed our wild pet. I mourned that it was unlikely we ever would have such a rare experience again. And yet, it was at the end of the week in which we lost Fanny that Merak, the human-imprinted red-tailed hawk, was released into our care in the park. Once again, and to a greater degree than before, we were to have the rare privilege of becoming acquainted with another relatively undomesticated creature. Our adventures with this magnificent and difficult raptor have been recorded in my second book, *A Wing in the Door*.

In the selection from *The View from Foley Mountain*, "The Rocks Remain", I wrote of the mutability of life. Living here has meant "living the changes". Over twenty years, I have seen fields turn into woods, a chain of ponds appear and a favourite pond die. Ravens fly where they never did before, and where a dozen bluebirds once nested, one solitary bird has lingered this year, sole survivor of a harsh spring.

The View from Foley Mountain is a young woman's book. I know now that there is a shadow over the beloved land here and indeed over the world. The web of life is assailed in so many directions that there is real doubt about the terms of our world's survival. And yet, this painful awareness makes each minute here more precious. Increasingly, through my husband Barry's experiences with his environmental education classes and my own conversations with many visitors, I am coming to see how passionately people everywhere and of all ages care about respecting and safeguarding nature. And, although I see the unbalances – the havoc wreaked by porcupines without predators, for example, and the trees assailed by ever more diseases and insects, I also see the healing that is possible. Within a year of the cessation of burning at the nearby municipal garbage dump, the lichens, indicators of air purity, were flourishing as they never had before.

I am still filled with wonder and delight by my life in the conservation area. With my sons gone, my solitude is profound now, allowing me to delve deeper into the world at my doorstep. Increasingly, I find a hunger to know, a need to hug so closely to the earth's line that I am wholly part of its essential mystery. Most of all, I find a need to discover and live with the sacredness inherent in all life and to continue to give in words what gift I can of the wonder that surrounds me.

About the author

Born and raised in a woods in Mississauga, Peri McQuay is the daughter of Canadian artists Ken Phillips and Marie Cecilia Guard. She has been writing professionally since 1980 and has been published extensively in Canada and the United States. As well as *The View From Foley Mountain*, she is the author of *A Wing in the Door: Adventures With a Redtailed Hawk*. Presently she is working on a biography of her parents, "The Magician's Daughter" and a sequel to *The View From Foley Mountain*, "A Foley Mountain Book of Days".

Photo by Alan Greene

About the artist

Jillian Hulme Gilliland has been drawing and painting since she was a child in Africa. She attended Natal University on a fine arts scholarship and taught high school before becoming botanical illustrator for Natal University. She and her husband travelled widely before setttling in Kingston, Ontario, where she gives art classes, illustrates books and works in water colour, pastel, inks and other media. Her work as an illustrator includes more than twenty books and the art for a syndicated feature, "Tell Me a Story," that appears in about 200 newspapers.